Biddy Baxter Edward Barnes and Rosemary Gill devised and wrote the Blue Peter Book

10s

Hello There!

This time last year we were asking ourselves a lot of questions.

Would Cindy, our second trainee guide dog puppy be as successful as her half sister, Honey?

Would we be able to think up another good scheme for helping other people at Christmas?

What could we do about the hundreds of people who were asking us 'Can't you possibly write some more "Blue Peter" books?'

Now, of course, we know the answers, and they've all turned out to be important achievements in the history of 'Blue Peter'.

Cindy *has* become as successful as Honey – so now, thanks to you, there are two 'Blue Peter' Guide Dogs for the Blind.

And because you sent us so many millions of parcels of wool and cotton, we were able to save

1

Do you recognize any of these photographs?

They've all been in 'Blue Peter'. Turn to the end for the answers.

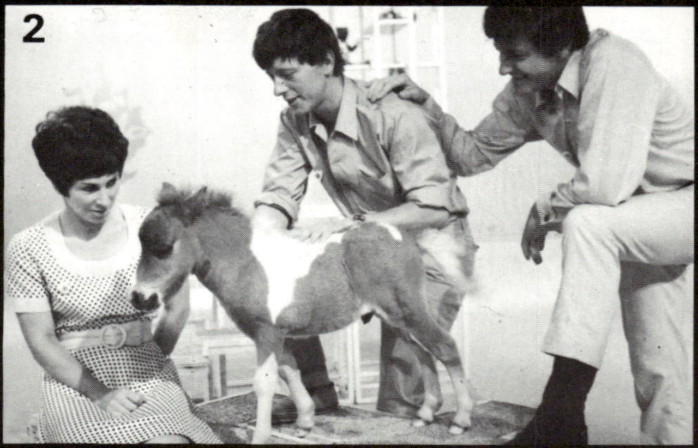

2

3

4

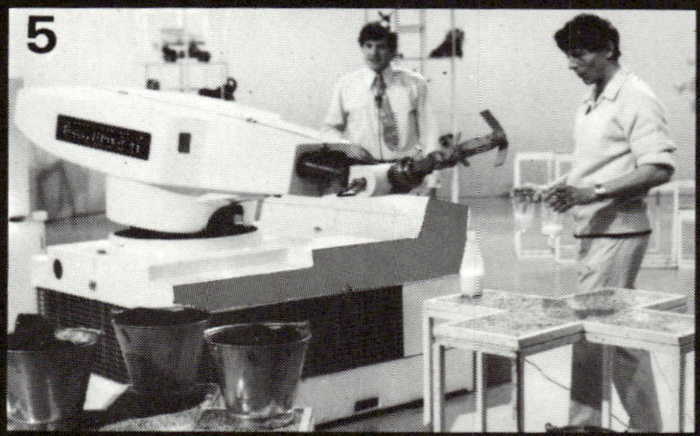

5

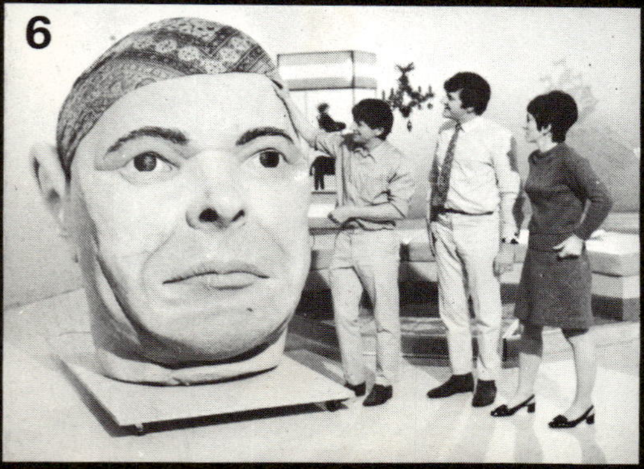

6

7

8

the lives of thousands of starving children in Biafra and Nigeria with our 'Blue Peter' Hospital Trucks and Emergency Doctors Cars.

As for the books – you've probably seen our 'Blue Peter' Minis. The first ones were published in March 1969. We've written Mini books about pets, television, our Safari to Morocco, and how to make Teddy Bear's clothes. Because you've suggested lots of other subjects, we're going to try and write more and more of them – so soon you should be able to build up a whole library of 'Blue Peter' Books.

In this, our newest book, you can read about Daniel who first appeared on the programme when he was only 14 weeks old – Free Fall Parachuting – Pavlova, the world's most famous ballerina – our tree felling expedition to Norway, and there are lots of things to make as well as stories about Paddington, Bleep & Booster and Bengo.

We hope you enjoy it, and good luck with the competition!

9

10

11

12

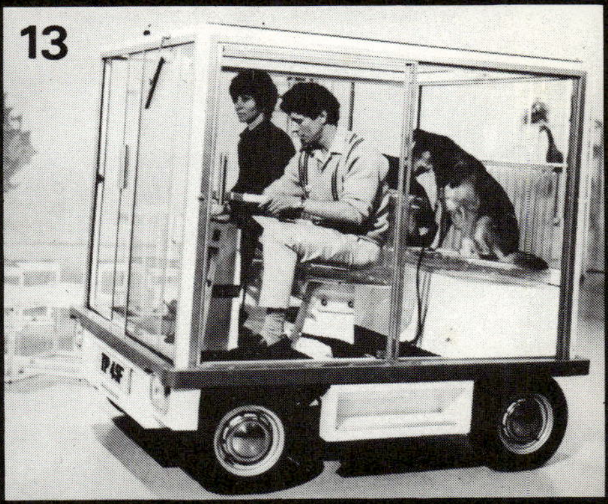
13

14

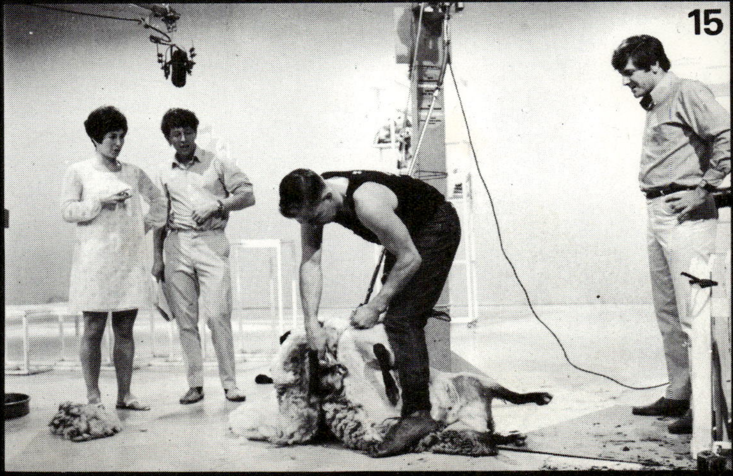
15

This poodle is expert at walking on her hind legs – but some tricks can be dangerous.

Tricks for Dogs

Do dogs enjoy them? Are they dangerous? How long should training sessions last?

If you're like us and lucky enough to have dogs as pets, you may long to teach them tricks that they can perform for you and in front of your friends. There are a good many simple commands such as 'sit and stay' and distance control that can appear to be tricks, although really they're part of your dog's basic training. And most dogs can be taught to 'shake hands' like Petra, or to 'die for the Queen' – which means you train your dog to flop down on to the floor.

Because all dogs need to be kept busy and occupied there's no reason why they shouldn't enjoy learning tricks, but it's vitally important to teach things suitable for the type of dog you're dealing with. Poodles, for instance, have strong springy limbs and can happily walk on their hind legs without coming to any harm, but it would be impossible – as well as cruel – to try to train a long, low slung dog such as a dachshund to walk on two legs. We know one dachshund, though, who puts on a marvellous rolling pin performance – rolling over and over with perfect ease, fifteen or twenty times without stopping. This is something that you couldn't possibly teach an Afghan or a Greyhound!

As well as relating the trick you want to teach your dog to the type of body he has, try and find out what his breed was originally used for. Hounds, for example, used their noses for hunting. Gun dogs and retrievers delight in hide and seek and fetching things. And as Staffordshire Bull Terriers were originally bred for fighting, it would be unwise to train one to perform an aggressive type of trick.

All the hunting breeds and greyhounds are fairly difficult to cater for, as they were bred for chasing

Patch catching a biscuit.

and killing, and this is something you obviously can't allow them to do. But what they can enjoy is catching things like biscuits, or doing low jumping. Do remember, though, that jumping is something you must be careful about teaching. It is not suitable for every breed. Racing greyhounds can jump over two or three low hurdles quite easily – but this would not be possible for a Corgi or a Sealyham.

If you ever throw anything for your dog to retrieve, make sure it's not small enough for him to swallow. Sometimes dogs have choked to death when they've swallowed small rubber balls or pebbles.

Sticks can be another pitfall. If, after they've been thrown, they fall upright in soft mud or earth, a dog running full tilt to retrieve it can be speared through his body or even through his eye or his mouth.

One of the safest things to throw is a rubber ring like the one Cindy has.

Some of the most intelligent dogs are mongrels – and probably the most amazing mongrel we've ever come across is Blackie who belongs to Mr. Zyla of Stoke-on-Trent. Mr. Zyla is Polish, and because he has taught him all his tricks in Polish, this is the only language Blackie understands. There is a perfect communication between them without Mr. Zyla ever raising his voice or getting angry.

Petra enjoys shaking hands.

Mr. Zyla tells Blackie to pick out a flag.

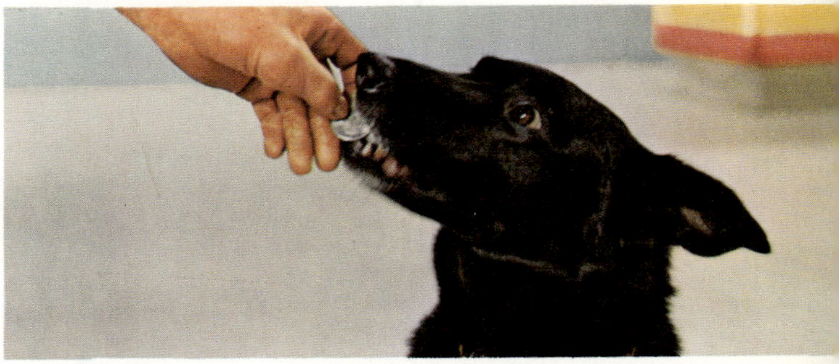

Blackie takes half a crown from John to buy a

bar of chocolate. Valerie gives Blackie the chocolate in exchange — he will not eat it without permission.

Khan, a Great Dane, said to be the only one of his breed in Britain to be trained to the police dog standard of obedience. Khan is practising with his owners, Keith and Denise Parsons.

When Blackie appeared on 'Blue Peter', he counted, played football, picked the correct flags out of a jumbled line up, and took half a crown from John – walked across the studio to Val – received a large bar of chocolate in exchange, which he held very carefully, and took back to John.

When you've decided what tricks are suitable for your dog, it's always best to start teaching him when he's as young as possible.

The first time you try it out, your dog will be baffled, but the more interesting you make the training sessions, the more keen he'll be to obey you. Remember to give him lots of praise and reward him whenever he does anything right – and stop the lessons as soon as he shows signs of becoming bored. A little and often is the golden rule, and remember to be enthusiastic about your commands. If you're not interested in the trick, you can't expect your dog to be!

Some people say that tricks are silly and futile and undignified. But this really shows a lack of understanding about their basic purpose. Tricks form an extremely useful purpose in building up a bond of communication between dog and owner, and can greatly increase understanding between them. Some dogs become desperately bored because their owners feel the best kind of life for them is one of complete freedom. This usually results in the dog becoming the menace of the neighbourhood. So, if you have a dog, make sure he gets plenty of attention and training – he'll have a much happier life, and be a far more rewarding pet!

I wouldn't do it for £1000–

that's what they say when you talk about free falling.

But most people don't get the chance to refuse. I was lucky. I was given the chance to accept.
When mountaineer, George Mallory was asked why on earth he wanted to climb Everest, he replied 'Because it was there.'
Every free faller knows just what he meant. It's the challenge. It's something you feel you've got to do – because somebody's asked you to do it.
But free falling isn't just a once in a life time.
When you've experienced that marvellous sensation of flying through the air – thousands of feet above the ground, you're hooked for life. At least, that's how it happened to me.
The first jump you ever make is on a 'static line', which means that your ripcord is on the end of a rope that is fastened to the aircraft. As you fall, the rope becomes taut and the ripcord is automatically pulled.
But the free faller pulls his own ripcord.
The length of time between leaving the aircraft and pulling the ripcord is known as the 'delay'. There's a five second delay – ten second delay – and so on, until you reach world class like Captain Joseph Kittingham of the US Army. He created a world record in 1960 when he stepped out of a balloon at 102,000 feet for a free fall of 84,700 feet – over 16 miles! His delay was 4 minutes 38 seconds.
Captain Kittingham had no need to worry – I wasn't going to challenge his record. If I could achieve a *five* second delay – ending with a fully opened parachute, I wouldn't be complaining!
I was lucky because I was trained by not one, but two of the best free fall teams in the world.
For all my initial training and my first static line jump, I went to the RAF Flying Falcons team at Abingdon. My Free Fall training, and my first five second delay were supervised by the Red Devils, the Army's Free Fall team.
Before you go anywhere near an aeroplane, there's a tremendous amount to be learnt about parachuting.
It took me a whole day just learning how to fall.
A parachutist hits the ground at the same speed as a man jumping off a 10 foot wall. And it's easy enough to break a leg from half that height – if you don't

know how to fall properly.

Then there's the control of the parachute in the air. Strung up in a practice harness, like a puppet dangling three feet above the ground, I learnt that by pulling on the rigging lines which control the amount of air entering the parachute canopy, and by swinging my body this way and that, it was possible to drop into a six foot circle on the ground from an aeroplane 5,000 feet in the air. Red Devil Brian David, my instructor, has hit a five inch disc from a height of 12,000 feet!

The moment of truth, when you actually climb out on to the wing of the aircraft and let go, is carefully rehearsed in a mock-up plane in the hangar.

It's important to get this bit right whilst you're still on the ground. When you're 5,000 feet up – there's no turning back for a second try.

As soon as I'd let go, I was to take up the static free fall position. This looks rather like a frog coming up for air. When falling at 120 mph, it's the only position which will stop you spinning and give you a chance to control your movements.

At last the big day arrived!

I was passed fit and capable for a five second delay. With five other Red Devils, I marched out of the briefing room and formed up in front of the waiting aircraft. Jumpmaster Bob Card checked our equipment. The free fall parachute was strapped on our backs; the reserve – in case the first one didn't open – was slung across our middles. On top of the reserve

1 On the wing of the mock-up plane in the hangar.

2 I learnt the right way to jump from an aircraft.

3 A final check on all our equipment was made by the Jumpmaster.

4 We climbed into the aircraft in reverse jumping orc

5 On the wing again, but this time I was 2,800 feet from the ground.

we carried an altimeter to check that we didn't run out of air.
The jump was from 2,800 feet.
The delay – five seconds.
Wind – Westerly, 8 knots.
My jumping position – No. 2.
We climbed aboard the De Havilland Rapide in reverse jumping order – and took off.
At 2,800 feet, Pilot Mike Watts cut out both engines. There was a sudden deafening silence, and I knew that this was it – there was no turning back now. We were formed up, crouching in jumping order, facing the stern of the aircraft.
The Jump master half rose and turned to face us. 'No. 1' he shouted.
And Corporal Ossie Power swung on to the wing – gave me a big grin – and disappeared.
'No. 2'.
That was me!
'Remember – as soon as you let go, start counting in thousands until you reach 1005 – then pull. OK?' I stepped out on to the wing, praying that I wouldn't forget what came after 1003.
'1001, 1002, 1003, 1004, a thousand and PULL! I looked up and saw my beautiful red and white canopy unfold in the sun. There was a jerk – and, suddenly everything seemed to stand still.
There was nothing between me and the earth– 2,000 feet below.
This was the life!

6 For five breathtaking seconds I fell through the air....

7 while Capt Shea-Simonds took pictures wearing this helmet camera.

8 I looked up and saw my canopy unfold in the sun.

9 When you reach the ground, there's only one thought in your mind. 'When will I make my next jump?'

'Dear Sir...'

Quills and parchment, sealing wax, seals and sand—this is just some of the equipment used by letter writers hundreds of years ago.

John de Warenne's Seal

Have you ever written to 'Blue Peter'? Each week, over three thousand letters arrive in our office. Sometimes they're written in pencil, but more usually with ball point or fountain pens. In the olden days though, things were quite different. Pens were made mostly from large goose quills – their nibs cut with small knives that came to be known as 'pen knives'. Ink pot stands had holes round their rims to take the quills and protect the delicate nibs.

Because blotting paper hadn't been invented, containers like giant pepper pots, filled with sand or fine pumice powder, were shaken over the letters.

After the powder had dried the ink, it was blown off and then the letter was almost ready to be sent away. But first it had to be sealed. Like blotting paper, gummed envelopes had yet to be invented, and as well as acting as a signature at the end of a letter, a seal was used on the outside to make sure the letter was not tampered with. If the person who received the letter found the seal unbroken, he knew no one but himself and the writer had read the contents.

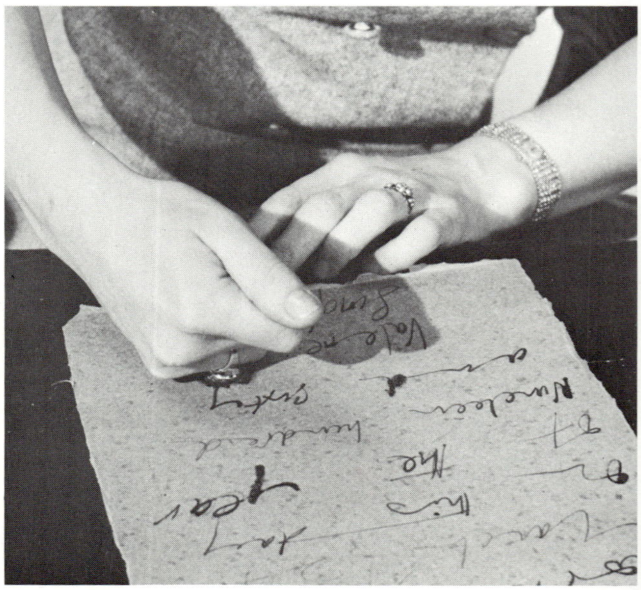

I'm using a ring to seal this letter. You can see an enlargement on the next page.

Signet rings were often used to make seals

This 'S' for Singleton seal belongs to me

William of Wykeham's Seal for New College, Oxford, and the silver die that made it.

Seals have been used on important documents for the last ten hundred years. They were made by pressing a mould or die of metal into hot wax. Sometimes the seal would be put straight on to the parchment, or else attached by a piece of ribbon or cord.

Kings and Queens had Great Seals that would appear on all State papers and documents such as treaties with foreign countries – and seals were also used by all important dignitaries and authorities. They were mostly round, and could be up to six inches in diameter, and they looked a bit like coins. They generally showed a crest or a shield, and had wording round the edge – often in Latin.

In 1851, when gummed envelopes were invented, the use of seals to fasten letters died out, but they are still used to this very day on important state and legal documents.

Looking at these pictures it seems as though great progress has been made since the days of parchment and quills. But soon writing itself may become old fashioned. Some people say that automatic dictating machines and typewriters will take the place of pen and paper – so maybe we'll return to using seals instead of signatures!

The Great Seal of Queen Elizabeth I

The Great Seal of Barbados.

FOOTBALL FAN

Are you a football fan too? With a home-made rattle like mine you can give your team some deafening applause every time they score. Make it from cheap off-cuts from a wood shop, and paint it in your team colours for a really professional finish.

1 To make the rattle you will need:
A piece of broom handle, 9″ long × 1″
4 blocks of wood, 2″ square × 1″ thick
2 pieces of wood, 9″ × 2″ × $\frac{1}{2}$″
2 pieces of plywood, 9″ × $\frac{3}{4}$″ × $\frac{1}{8}$″

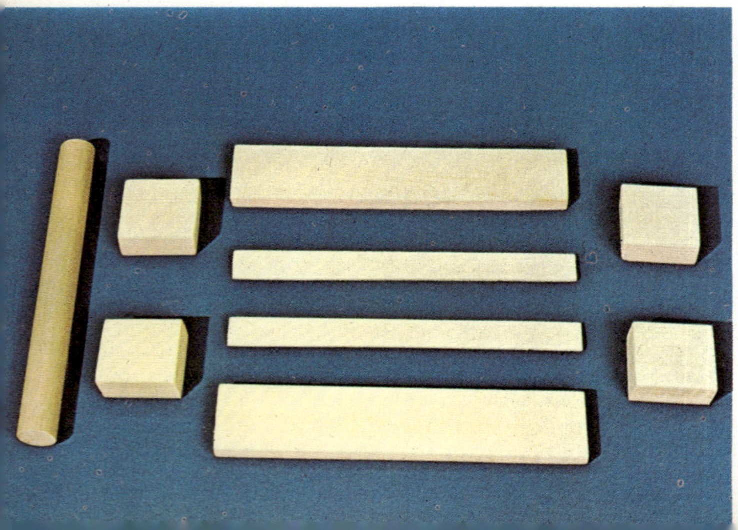

2 With a drill the same diameter as the broom handle, make a hole through the centre of two of the square blocks of wood.

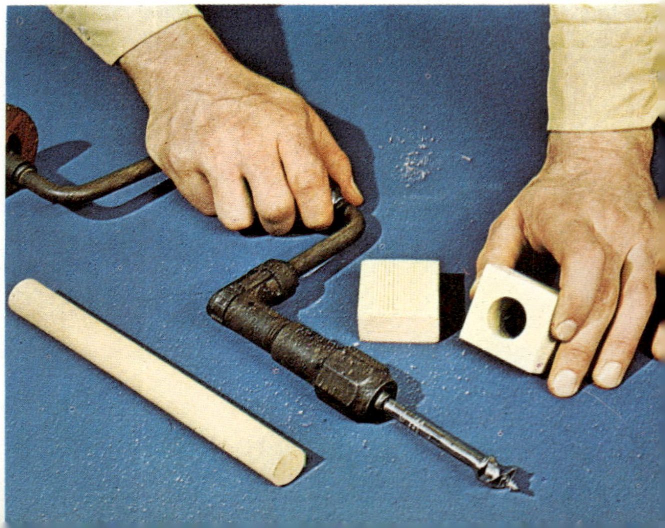

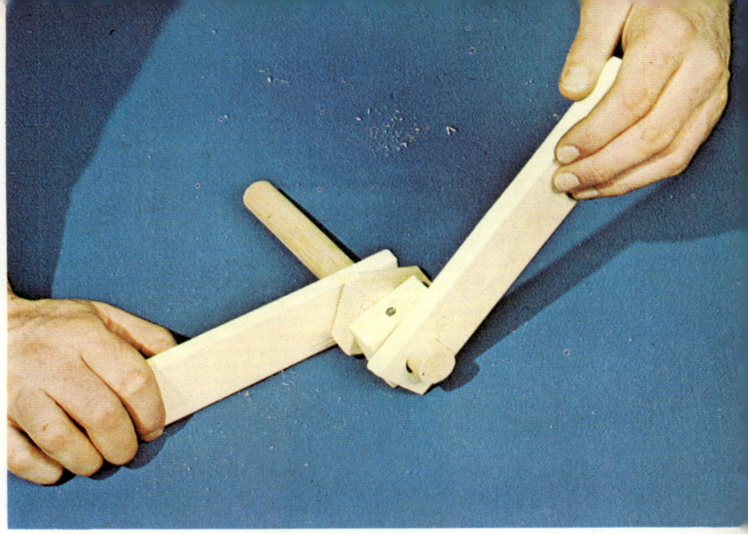

3 Push the squares over the broom handle so that the corner of one block is across the flat side of the other. If necessary glue and screw to the handle for a tight fit.

4 Drill a hole at one end of each of the two flat pieces of wood. They should spin freely when you fit them on the handle.

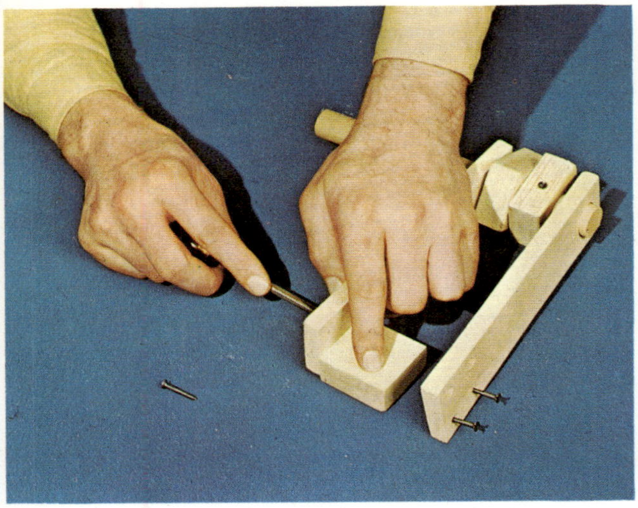

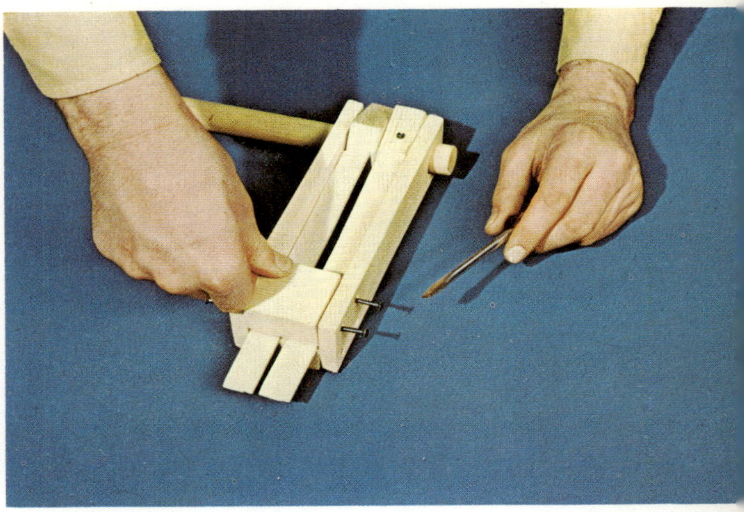

5 After testing for spin, fix them apart with one of the 2″ × 2″ × 1″ blocks of wood. Make sure you screw the block flush to the edges of the top and bottom pieces of wood.

6 Lay the two strips of plywood on the block and sandwich them in place with the second block. Test for maximum rattle.

7 Screw right through the top block into the second block to keep the plywood firmly in place. Trim off the ends of the plywood.

8 Paint the rattle in your team's colours. Mine's blue and white because I'm a Spurs supporter.

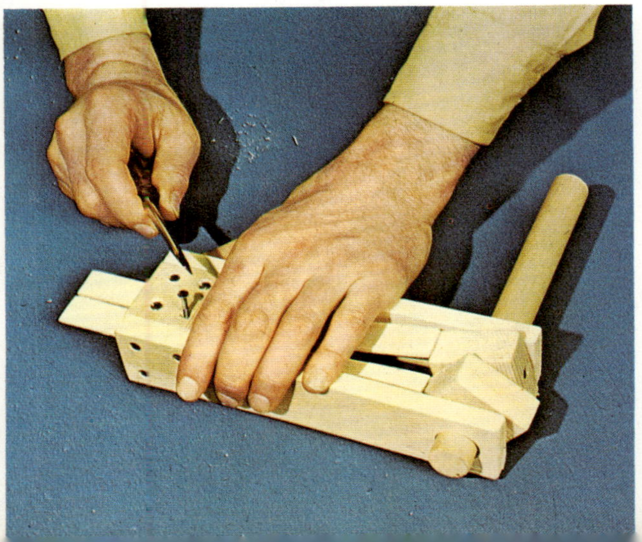

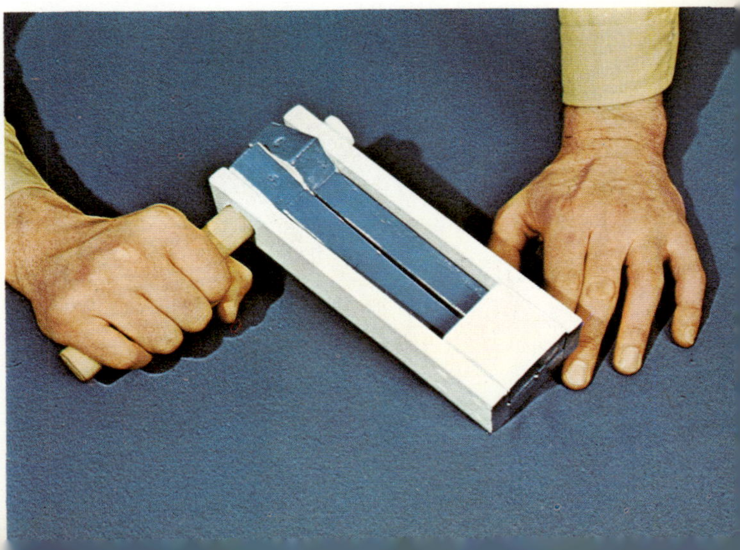

The F.A. Cup

One March day, twenty-two men wearing long white trousers and caps walked out onto the field at the Kennington Oval. Were they going to play a Test Match? No, they were not! They were about to play the very first Cup Final ever. The date was 1872, and the two teams were Wanderers and the Royal Engineers. Two thousand spectators paid a shilling each to see Wanderers win 1 – 0, and if you'd been one of the spectators in that crowd, you'd scarcely have recognised the game you were watching as football.

To begin with, there were no goal nets. Two posts with a tape stretched from one to the other marked the goalmouth – and every time a goal was scored, the team changed ends.

There was no neatly marked field, for in those days there was no centre circle, no half way line, and no goal and penalty areas – just ropes to keep the enthusiastic fans well away from the pitch.

If the ball went out of play, both sides made a dash for it. It didn't matter which team had kicked it out, the throw in went to whichever team grabbed the ball first.

You wouldn't have seen the neat, accurate, cross

Goal ! Wanderers slam the ball between the posts and the F.A. Cup is won for the very first time.

field passing that skilled players use today. It simply hadn't been invented. In those days, the game was played with eight forwards and three defenders, and the way to score was for one of the forwards to dribble the ball up the field, backed up by one of his team mates to fend off the opposition or take the ball if things got too hot.

Watching a game like this may not sound like a very exciting Saturday afternoon, but the crowd who attended that very first Cup Final waved and cheered just as they do today.

The Cup that the Wanderers won at that first final was nothing like the splendid trophy that is fought for today. Football wasn't a rich sport in those Victorian days. There were only 15 teams in the newly formed Football Association and all the players were amateurs. Their teams had a whip round to collect money to buy a trophy and they managed to scrape together £20. With the money, they bought a little silver cup, with two handles and a footballer on top. It may not have been much to look at, but for the teams in the Football Association it was a treasure beyond price. By the 1880's enthusiasm for football had spread all over the country. At the cup

'Is that t'cup ? Why, it's more like a tea kettle !'

final of 1883, Blackburn Olympic beat Old Etonians 2 – 1, and for the very first time the Cup went North. Brass bands played and cheering crowds lined the pavements as the team drove through the streets in a wagonette drawn by six horses. Just like today, Warburton, the Blackburn Olympic Captain, held the Cup high for the crowds to see. 'Is that t'coop?' shouted a voice from the crowd. 'Why, it's like a tea kettle.'

'Aye, lad,' shouted back Warburton. 'But it's welcome in Lancashire and it'll ne'er go back to Lunnon!'

And it never did.

Year after year the Cup was won by teams from the North or the Midlands, and in 1895 Aston Villa won the Cup and took it back in triumph to Birmingham. Then a man called Mr. Shillcock who made footballs and football boots asked if he could display the cup in his shop window. The team agreed and people flocked to Mr. Shillcock's shop to see the Trophy. But on the morning of 12th September, 1895, when Mr. Shillcock took down the shutters he was horrified to find the cup had gone! It was practically a national disaster. The newspapers were full of stories of the theft, police and detectives searched high and low, there was even a £10 reward offered for information, but nobody came forward. The Football Association Challenge Cup had vanished into thin air, and it was never seen again.

The scene of the crime—Mr. Shillcock's Football Shop, Birmingham.

The 'tea kettle'–stolen in 1895 and never seen again.

£10 REWARD.

STOLEN!

From the Shop Window of W. Shillcock, Football Outfitter, Newtown Row, Birmingham, between the hour of 9-30 p.m. on Wednesday, the 11th September, and 7-30 a.m., on Thursday, the 12th inst., the

ENGLISH CUP,

the property of Aston Villa F.C. The premises were broken into between the hours named, and the Cup, together with cash in drawer, stolen.

The above Reward will be paid for the recovery of the Cup, or for information as may lead to the conviction of the thieves.

Information to be given to the Chief of Police, or to Mr. W. Shillcock, 73, Newtown Row.

A replica was made, but it somehow didn't seem to have the same appeal as the original. So in 1911 a new and splendid trophy was made.

It was bigger than the 'tea kettle' and much more handsome. It was 19 inches high, and it cost 50 guineas to make. Today the F.A. Cup is priceless.

It was a great day for us when the Football Association allowed us to show the Cup on 'Blue Peter.' On a silver band round the plinth are inscribed the names and dates of all the cup winners since the Football Association was formed. Today over 600 clubs battle through the knock-out competition, and as I picked it up and thought of all the famous footballers who had held this Cup before me, I knew I had in my hands a piece of football history.

Mystery Picture

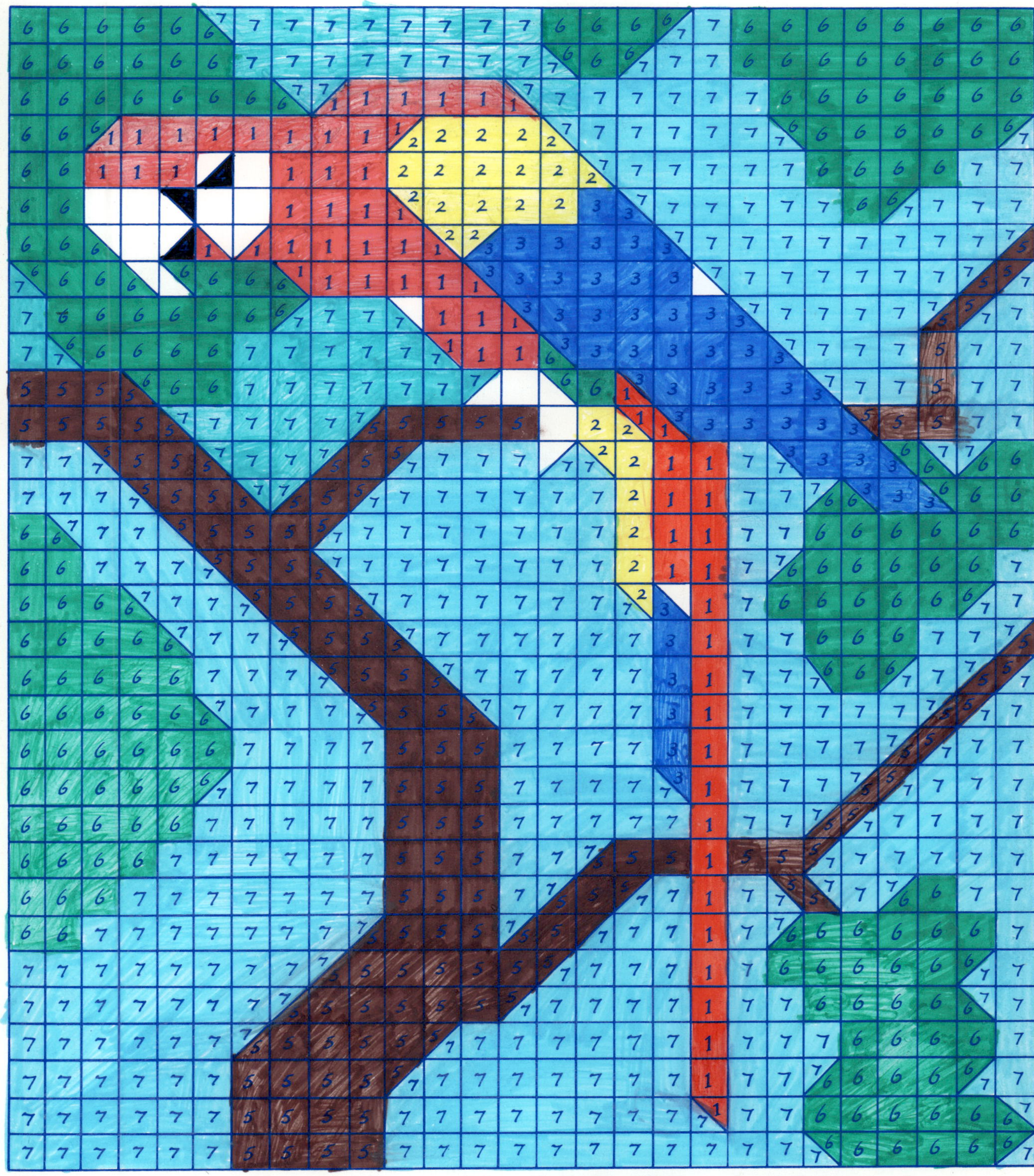

Colour the spaces as indicated by the numbers and the mystery picture will appear. 1 Red; 2 Yellow; 3 Dark Blue; 4 Black; 5 Brown; 6 Green; 7 Light Blue.

Five months old – Daniel's muscles are developing, and like all babies, he has a very firm grip.

Six weeks old – At this age Daniel just sleeps, eats and cries. His feet are as tiny as matchboxes.

Daniel Grows Up

September 30th, 1968, was a very important day for us on 'Blue Peter'—it was when Daniel Simon Scott made his first appearance on the programme and he was only fourteen weeks old!

Since then Daniel's taken part in dozens of Blue Peter's and we've been able to watch him grow and develop, and turn into a real personality. But unless you have a baby brother or sister of your own, it's difficult to realise just how helpless human beings are when they're first born. We hoped that by having Daniel on the programme, we could show how babies are looked after and how very different they are from animals' babies. All Daniel could do for his first few weeks of life was to eat, sleep, and cry when he wanted something. But baby wildebeest can actually stand up when they're only a few *minutes* old, and puppies and kittens can fend for themselves when human babies are still quite helpless.

Daniel has seven brothers and sisters so he's used to lots of people around him, and living at a busy rectory, he's used to plenty of visitors, too. In fact, our 'Blue Peter' studio must have seemed very quiet and peaceful compared with life at home.

Some people think that looking after a baby is a job for girls – but we don't agree. We've thoroughly enjoyed bathing Daniel – dressing and feeding him – playing with him and taking him out for walks – especially since he began to react to us and to his surroundings.

Bringing up a small baby takes a good deal of patience, but it's very rewarding. We think Daniel, our 'Blue Peter' Baby, is well worth it!

Eight months old – Now Daniel is beginning to be able to concentrate. He was fascinated by this giant Newton's Cradle.

Nine months old – Daniel's favourite toys are Mr. Barnes his Teddy Bear, and this old tin.

Nine months old – Daniel's smile of recognition – he knows many people now, not only members of his family.

Ten months old – Daniel plays quite happily on his own now – but we make sure we never leave him alone with Barney.

The Case of the Hi-jacked Horse

Can you solve this case? Five careless mistakes gave away the crooks. Peter spotted them. Can you?

The sun was shining as Detective Sergeant McCann and his nephew Bob took their places in the Grandstand at the International Horse Show. McCann was enjoying a well earned holiday and looking forward to the most exciting event in show jumping – the competition for the priceless Wellborough Trophy.

The afternoon promised to be exciting. Wild Rose, ridden by Whitby Stevens, had had a marvellous season, but there was unknown competition from the USA. Being flown from the States, especially for this event, was Nice Teddy. He'd never been seen in British show jumping circles, but he'd had a tremendous coast-to-coast success in America. By all accounts he presented a formidable challenge to Wild Rose.

Suddenly a voice came over the tannoy:

'Ladies and Gentlemen. We are sorry to inform you that the start of the Wellborough Trophy will be delayed owing to the late arrival of the plane bringing Nice Teddy from the United States.'

On a road from the airport, a horsebox was speeding towards the stadium. At the wheel was Brick McKinsey, the owner and trainer of Nice Teddy, and sitting by his side studying a route map was champion rider Elliot Eastower.

'Take it easy, Mr. McKinsey' said Eastower, 'we should turn off soon – don't let's miss the sign.'

Two miles ahead, three masked men were hastily planting a false sign that read 'To the Stadium'. A few quick blows with a hammer and their work was done. Hurriedly, they ducked behind the hedge and settled down to wait.

'There's the sign,' he cried, and turned off down a narrow lane. It got narrower and narrower until at last they were confronted by a huge stone wall.

'This road don't seem to go no place, sir' said Eastower.

'Maybe we'd better back up and try again.'

'You're not going to try anything again,' hissed a voice in his ear. Elliot turned to be confronted by a masked man. He felt a pain in his head, saw a flash of multi-coloured stars and then blackness.

Within seconds Eastower and McKinsey lay bound and gagged in the straw of the horse box, while Nice Teddy whinnied disconsolately. The masked man waved his arm and from a narrow turning up the lane another identical horsebox appeared. Roughly, Nice Teddy was transferred and the hi-jacked horse was once more heading towards the stadium.

'Do you think we'll get away with it?' questioned the first masked man.

'There's nothing to it!' said the fat man with the cigar. 'All you've got to do is to make sure that Nice Teddy *loses* this competition and Wild Rose will win. For the money Whitby Stevens is paying us, that's not too much to ask!'

Back at the Horse Show the strains of Oklahoma drew to an end as the announcer said: 'Ladies and Gentlemen. We're pleased to announce that Nice

Teddy has just arrived and the competition can begin.'

One after another the best horses and riders in the show jumping world scored fault after fault. The course was a killer. As Bob and his uncle watched the competition, a large man smoking a big cigar sat down beside them.

'Pardon me. Do you mind if I sit here? I've just got in from the States in time to watch my horse competing for the Wellborough Trophy.'

Bob took a quick look in his programme.

'Are you Mr. Brick McKinsey then?' asked Bob.

'None other – it's my first time ever in this wonderful country and it's going to be a great day for me. When Nice Teddy wins, back home they'll be celebrating as though it's the 3rd of July!'

'I believe your plane was late,' said Sergeant McCann.

'Er – yes,' said the bogus McKinsey. 'There was so much fog at Kennedy Airport in Washington that we were delayed more than an hour.'

Now came the moment everyone was waiting for as Whitby Stevens cantered into the ring on Wild Rose.

'This is it,' whispered Bob, nudging his uncle.

The silence was broken by a bell as Wild Rose passed through the electric timer and approached the first fence which she cleared with inches to spare. Two long strides and she soared over the five barred gate and took the water jump in her stride. There was just one fence to go – could she do it? Whitby Stevens leant forward in the saddle as they approached the great double spread. Wild Rose cleared the first part, but her hind foot just caught the last bar. It wobbled for a moment and there was a great 'Ooh!' from the crowd as the bar rolled on to the ground.

'Four faults for Whitby Stevens on Wild Rose,' came the voice from the tannoy.

Whitby Stevens looked tight lipped as he patted his horse's steaming neck.

'And now the last horse to jump – Nice Teddy, ridden by Elliot Eastower – both appearing for the first time in this country.'

'That's my boy!' grinned McKinsey.

Silence fell on the arena. Only a clear round would give the American the Trophy. Beside them, Brick McKinsey bit deep into his cigar.

Nice Teddy started well and cleared the first three fences without much trouble, but to everyone's astonishment, when he came to the five barred gate, he stopped dead in his tracks.

'Holy Cow!' rasped McKinsey.

'Nice Teddy collects three faults for a refusal,' boomed the tannoy.

'Now there's only one point in it,' muttered Bob, tensely, but the American didn't answer.

Elliot Eastower brought Nice Teddy round for a second attempt. This time he didn't refuse, but leapt forward and crashed straight into it. Then followed a trail of destruction! Nice Teddy seemed to have gone berserk – striped poles littered the arena and hedges crashed to the ground.

'Nice Teddy has 23 faults!' came the voice over the tannoy.

'Gosh!' said Bob, turning to the American – but he had already left the grandstand.

Thunderous applause greeted the presentation of the priceless Wellborough Trophy to Whitby Stevens, and afterwards Whitby Stevens and Brick McKinsey were interviewed for Television by Grandstand reporter, Barney Coalport. After he'd congratulated the winner, the commentator turned to McKinsey –

'I suppose you must be feeling very disappointed. What are your next plans?'

'I still think Nice Teddy's a great jumper, so I'm entering him for your famous steeplechase – the Derby.'

'And now for the winner. What are your comments Mr. Stevens?'

'Well, when I met Brick and Elliot at Badminton last week, I hardly dared hope that things would turn out like this!'

Coalport turned to McKinsey and held out the mike.

'And one last word from our gallant loser.'

'Well, I'm just off to give Nice Teddy a big bucket of cold water,' said McKinsey. 'He's just as hot and thirsty as if he'd won!'

'Better luck next time,' said Coalport – and was just about to shake hands when to Bob's embarrassment, Detective Sergeant McCann broke into the group.

'There'll be no next time for either of you,' barked McCann.

Quickly, Coalport signalled to the cameras.

'We now return you to the Grandstand studio,' he announced hastily – and cut the interview. Angrily he turned on McCann.

'How dare you interrupt my interview?' he demanded.

'You've missed the scoop of a lifetime,' replied McCann, as he snapped the handcuffs on Stevens and McKinsey.

'Take care of the Wellborough Trophy, Bob. The stadium police are already holding Elliot Eastower.'

'But . . . I don't understand,' stammered Bob. McCann turned to him.

'The three of them are involved in a plot. Whitby Stevens wanted that Trophy, and he didn't care how he got it.'

'How on earth did you know?' Bob demanded.

'They made five very foolish mistakes,' smiled McCann, 'and now all three of them are for the high jump!'

Did you spot the mistakes? Peter did. **Check your answers on page 76.**

CHIEF OF THE NOAKIS!

Do you want to join my tribe?

For dressing up, or for a fancy dress competition, an Indian outfit is the easiest of the lot. All you need are some jeans, strings of beads, some makeup and a few feathers. Make a headdress from a strip of corrugated card and push feathers in the holes. Give yourself some terrifying war paint — if you can't get hold of any theatrical make-up like mine, you could use bright red lipstick and black eyeliner (you get it off again with cold cream!).

If you're going to be a Noaki in the winter, make sure you're going somewhere warm. It's very easy to turn from a Redskin into a Blueskin!

BLEEP and BOOSTER

'Look Bleep,' cried Booster, rushing into the room where Bleep was just about to have tea. 'Look what I've invented!' He held out a very odd looking gun. It was home made from springs and coils and Booster was very proud of it. 'What's it supposed to be?' asked Bleep, 'an earth man's mousetrap?' and he laughed as he turned back to his favourite tea, hot buttered stellar paste sandwiches and a steaming mug of Asteroidade. Booster was furious. 'It's a Sonic Solidifying Gun,' he snapped. 'There isn't another one like it in the world. Or in space for that matter!' He took careful aim at Bleep's mug and fired. There was a high pitched whine and instantly the mug split and out on to the table fell a frozen lump of Asteroidade. By now both boys had lost their tempers.

'Go away,' cried Bleep 'and take your mousetrap with you!'

Booster stormed out to the landing strip where the space pod he shared with Bleep lay parked under the shadow of Space Freighter 9. He stowed his Sonic Solidifying Gun carefully on board, climbed in and blasted off.

'Mousetrap indeed,' he muttered as he adjusted the controls and roared off into space.

That night, the Miron City Space Centre was in a state of emergency. Booster had not returned and all eyes were glued to the scanner screens watching for a sign of Booster's missing space pod. Suddenly the Space Traffic Controller leaned forward and pointed at a faint trace on the scanner.

'There he goes,' he cried.

'Where? Where?' cried Bleep.

'He is in deadly danger,' said the Space Controller. 'He has been drawn into irresistible orbit by the most deadly planet in the galaxy – Gelatanus X.' 'Quick,' ordered the Captain, 'All Miron Commandos to the Space Fleet. Booster must be headed off.'

Alarm sirens blared out across Miron City as the high speed rescue operation began. Inside Space Freighter 9 the Captain wrestled to make radio contact with the tiny space pod, while Bleep sat next to him, tense with worry. He had heard of Gelatanus X and he knew that unless Booster could be overtaken, the little space pod would be sucked down into the spongy surface of the planet where the terrible jelly-like Gelatanoid monsters lurked.

Suddenly a faint voice came over the loud-speaker –

'Emergency, Emergency – this is Booster – Emergency, Emergency.'

Over and over again the message was repeated, and now the little spaceship appeared on the screen.

'We have found him,' cried Bleep. 'Now he can be saved!'

But at that instant the radio went dead – they saw the little ship take a sudden downward plunge – and before their horrified eyes it sank towards Gelatanus X, closer and closer to the spongy crust!

But the space pod didn't sink. It was too light and floated precariously on its landing pads. There was still a chance! Now the Mirons could see Booster's frightened face on the screen and from the windows of Space Freighter 9 could be seen the sinister shapes of the Gelatanoids as they slithered towards the trapped boy.
'Now hear this,' barked the Captain. 'The Space Commandos cannot land and nor can I. We are all too heavy and would sink immediately we touched the surface.' He turned to Bleep.
'Only you can save your friend. You are small and light. You are his only hope. Hurry!'
He thrust two ray guns into Bleep's hands and settled a jet pack on his shoulders.
'Good luck my son,' he said, as he helped Bleep through the hatch. 'We must trust to luck that there will be enough power in one jet pack to get you both back safely. You must carry no excess weight, or your life will be in danger, too.'
For a moment, Bleep hung back, but one look at the Gelatanoids made up his mind. 'Goodbye father' he gulped, and bravely stepped out into space. As he landed, Bleep could see the Gelatanoids piling up against the space pod. Quickly he opened fire and in the ray gun's blast the monsters began to melt. 'Open up Booster,' yelled Bleep, and with his finger on the trigger, he blasted his way through to the hatch on the space pod's roof. Thankfully he dropped inside.
'Oh Bleep,' cried Booster. 'I thought you would never come.'
'No time for thanks now,' gasped Bleep as he handed his friend the second ray gun. 'Look! The Gelatanoids are beginning to ooze through the airlocks!'
Both boys opened fire – then suddenly, Bleep's gun packed up. He had used so much power blasting his way into the space pod that his ray gun was useless. By now the cabin was clear again, so quickly they checked the fire-power meter on Booster's gun.
'Only 800 gamma power left,' said Booster anxiously. 'Is that enough?'
'Enough to fend off one more attack,' gulped Bleep, 'but not enough to get us through the hatch and back to the Space Freighter 9.'
'What can we do?' asked Booster. 'I can't think of a plan.'
'I know,' cried Bleep. 'Your radio is broken, but I can call for help.' Quickly he spun the control knob on his jacket and back in Space Freighter 9 the Captain heard the call sign.
'Bleep – bleep. Our guns useless. Bleep – bleep, request supporting fire for our escape. Bleep – bleep – over and out.'
Tensely the boys waited and within seconds the cabin flashed with blinding light as the space commandos opened fire from Space Freighter 9 hovering overhead.
With a searing sizzle the Gelatanoids sprawling over the space pod dropped off and melted, but then, to the boys' horror, they felt their ship begin to move.
'We're sinking,' moaned Bleep. 'The fire power was too strong. The planet is melting, too!'
The poor boys huddled together as the cabin grew darker and darker as the portholes sank gradually below the surface.
'This is goodbye Booster,' gulped Bleep and held out his hand in a last farewell.
'No, it isn't!' cried Booster. 'There's just one last chance', and he grabbed his Sonic Solidifying Gun from under the seat.
'Quick, Bleep – don't give up! The roof hatch is our last chance, there's just time to open it.'
Urgently they forced it open and scrambled through.

Desperately Booster opened fire. At first nothing happened, but then there was a screaming whine from the gun, and like magic, the watery relics of the Gelatanoids froze solid, and soon Booster had frozen enough monsters for them to stand on.
They were just in time, for now there was nothing to be seen of the space pod – just the surface of Gelatanus X seething like boiling porridge.

'Hang on to my feet,' cried Bleep as he switched his jet pack to ignition. 'We'll get back to Space Freighter 9 yet – if our luck holds out.'
And it did. Safely inside the Space Freighter 9 they sank down exhausted.
'We got back thanks to your splendid invention,' said Bleep. 'I am sorry I laughed at your Sonic Solidifying Gun.'
'And you risked your life to save me,' said Booster. 'If I hadn't lost my temper, I would never have got in such danger.'
We must never quarrel again they agreed and settled down by the porthole with a steaming mug of Asteroidade each to watch for the friendly lights of Miron City.

TINSEL SWEET TREES

These sparkling Christmas trees are special ones because you can eat all the decorations! They are sweets wrapped in bright cellophane. When you've eaten all the decorations you can save the trees and refill them next year with fresh sweets.

To make my big tree I used: 12 inch length $\frac{1}{4}$ inch dowelling; a yogurt tub; cellulose filler; coloured cellophane; aluminium foil; gold foil paper; cardboard; tinsel; sticky tape; glue; sweets; and this is how I did it.

1 The trunk of the tree is a piece of dowelling. Fill a yogurt or cream tub three-quarters full with cellulose filler. If you haven't any filler, use modelling clay. Push the stick into the filler and leave to set firm.

2 Next cover the tub with gold foil paper and then with a layer of red cellophane. A little glue will hold the cellophane in place. Make sure that you have washed the tub well.

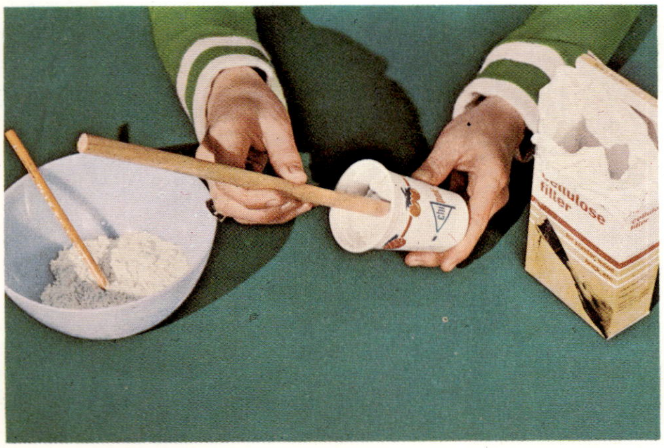

3 The cone shape of the tree is made from thin cardboard. A compass helps to get the correct shape which looks like an open fan. Cut a small piece from the top point. Bend the cardboard round into the cone shape and secure with sticky tape.

4 Cut a piece of foil paper the same shape as the cone but slightly bigger. Cover the cone with this paper. There is no need to glue the foil in place. Just wrap the foil round the cone and tuck the ends in firmly top and bottom.

---

5 I used about $\frac{3}{4}$ lb. boiled sweets to cover this tree, but if you use smaller sweets you may need a few more. To make shiny decorations cover the sweets with a layer of aluminium foil and then with coloured cellophane. Twist the ends into a 'tail'.

6 Cut 'X' shaped slits in the cone about half an inch from the bottom and about two inches apart. Push 'tails' of sweets into slits. Carry on round and up the cone putting in less sweets with each round. Finish off with a sweet pushed in the top hole.

---

7 Fix a strand of tinsel inside the cone with sticky tape. Wind the tinsel below the first row of sweets, then up round the lines of sweets to the top. A dab of glue will stop it unwinding again.

8 You can make a tiny version of the tree using small sweets wrapped in clear cellophane. A cotton reel makes a tub and a pencil a trunk. Little sweets get eaten fast, so make sure you have plenty handy to refill your tree!

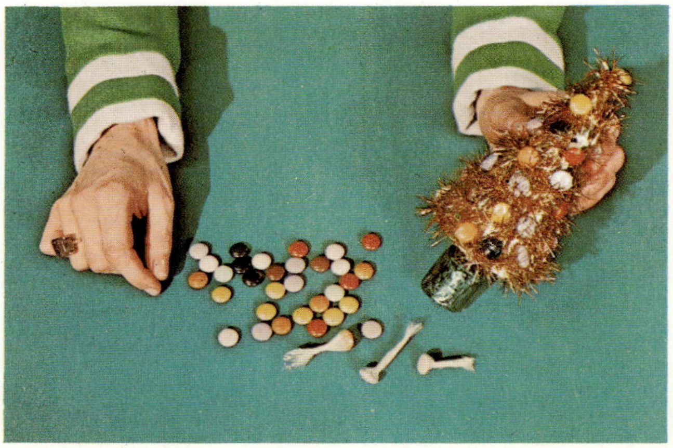

Present from Norway

'You know that Christmas tree that they put up in Trafalgar Square,' said John. 'Well–somebody's got to chop it down–so why don't we?' A few days after that remark, John and Peter packed two large axes and boarded SAS Flight 518 outward bound for Oslo.

In 1946 the grateful people of Oslo gave the people of London a great Christmas tree hewn from the forest of Oslo. The tree was to say 'thank you' for the hospitality London had given to Norwegian soldiers, sailors and airmen during the war. That was 23 years ago – but it didn't end with Christmas 1946. Every Christmas ever since, a tree has been cut down from the same forest and sailed up the Oslo Fjord bound for London Docks and Trafalgar Square. It has become a tradition – and the generous Norwegians love a tradition every bit as much as we do.

The tradition of the Christmas tree has only been in England for about 125 years. Before that, all our festivities were held round a huge Yule log which was lit on Christmas Eve and blazed away all through Christmas Day.

But in 1840 the young German Prince Albert of Saxe-Coburg married Queen Victoria of England. They had a large family – and enjoyed a large family Christmas together. But Albert missed the fir tree that had always formed the centre of the Christmas celebrations when he was a boy in Germany. So one Christmas he gave his children their first Christmas tree.

We had 'Forest Coffee' with the Mayor of Oslo before we started.

Half an hour's chopping made only a small dent in the massive tree.

News of the tree leaked out, and soon every family in England bought a fir tree and decorated it with toys and tinsel for Christmas Day.

The Christmas tree forest in Oslo had snow on the ground when we first arrived, but it was pelting with rain. The tree was enveloped by swirling fog—and from beneath its ghostly branches loomed a figure in black wearing a great gold chain. It turned out to be the Lord Mayor of Oslo, who was very friendly and spoke in fluent English. He had come to take the first ceremonial chop at the tree – but before we started we were introduced to another Norwegian custom – 'Forest Coffee'. This is made in an enormous black kettle on a roaring wood fire – and served with delicious waffles. With the temperature just on freezing and our boots full of slush, it was very welcome.

After half an hour of chopping, no one was complaining about the cold. We were only about one-tenth of the way through the trunk when Bjôrn arrived with his automatic saw. We had originally intended to cut it all down by hand – but the sight of the gleaming new machine made us weaken. Under Bjôrn's expert guidance, we went through the three-foot trunk in just under two minutes.

But there was no cry of 'Timber!' as the great pine crashed to the ground. The top of the tree was lashed to the jib of a roaring crane. There was a moment when the whole tree gave a tremendous shudder – and then slowly, very slowly and gently,

Then Bjôrn arrived with his automatic saw –

– and we had the tree down in less than two minutes.

The tree was loaded on to an enormous truck – and under Police Escort, we drove through the city of Oslo –

– until we reached the docks where the tree was swung aboard M.V. Baltique.

Ten days later, after its journey across the North Sea, we pulled the tree into Trafalgar Square.

the whole 30 feet of it was lowered majestically to the ground.

Per Finstad, the 6 foot 2 inch Forest Manager, watched anxiously. He hadn't broken a branch on a London tree in 22 years – and he didn't want his first disaster to be watched by the 'Blue Peter' cameras.

But at last, with every branch and fir cone intact, the tree was taken under Police escort to the Oslo docks and swung aboard M.V. *Baltique*.

We watched as she vanished into the mist of the Oslo Fjord and headed towards the North Sea for England.

Ten days later John and I were standing in Trafalgar Square. It was 7 o'clock on a cold, dark, foggy morning. The fog seemed to have followed us all the way from Norway. The tree had survived its journey across the North Sea, and was being brought up that morning from London Docks. (The 1958 tree was broken clean in two by a force 10 gale – but the kind Norwegians hastily chopped down a replacement and sent it over the following week).

Now at the far end of Whitehall, we picked out the blue flashing lights of the Police motor-cycle escort – as they waved the early London traffic to one side to make way for the tree. Lying stretched out overhanging the lorry, it looked like a strange green monster, angrily swishing its tail as the procession swung into the Square.

John and I joined a team from Westminster City Council and began the enormous task of putting the tree up again. And that's every bit as tricky as chopping it down – with one important difference. If we broke it this time, it was an awful long way to go back for another one! And what would Mr. Finstad say?

We split into two teams. The idea was for the first team to winch the tree into an upright position, whilst the second team guided the base of the trunk into the hole.

John and I joined the winch gang until Mick, the Irish foreman, said:

'You're a big fella. We need more weight on the bottom of the tree.'

I didn't know whether that was a compliment or not, but I went to join the heavy gang, and heaved and shoved until at last the trunk slipped safely down into the special hole. That hole was made 23 years ago to receive the very first tree from Norway. It's only used once a year, and for the rest of the time it lies hidden under a flagstone.

The tree was up! As we left the electricians moved in and began to wire up the 600 electric bulbs ready for the official switch on.

But 'Blue Peter' hadn't finished yet.

Ten days later it was Val's turn.

They needed some weight at the base of the tree so they picked me. I can't imagine why!

John and I were at the front of a huge crowd that had turned out to watch the Ceremony of Switching on the lights.

A large wooden platform was crammed with Very Important People.

The Press photographers jostled for position firing off a barrage of flash bulbs. As well as our own 'Blue Peter' cameras there was a battery of news cameras; and live outside broadcast cameras from ITV!

The Lord Mayor of Westminster made a speech and introduced:–

'His Excellency the Ambassador for Norway' – who made a speech and introduced:–

'Miss Valerie Singleton of Blue Peter'.

There was a great fanfare of trumpets – and H.E. the Norwegian Ambassador together with Miss Valerie Singleton of Blue Peter pressed the button that switched on 600 white lights which said:

'A Happy Christmas from the people of Oslo to the people of London'.

Before a battery of press, film and T.V. cameras, Val joined the Norwegian Ambassador to switch on the lights.

NEWSPAPER TRICKS

From one newspaper you can make a whole jungle of trees, or ladders six feet long, or even Magic Rings. To make these newspaper tricks you'll need a pair of scissors and some sticky tape—but don't even try to make the Objects! They're impossible!

How to make trees

1 Roll up a sheet of newspaper and cut one end into strips.

2 Holding the end loosely, pull out the centre strips and the tree will 'grow'.
Fasten the trunk with a piece of sticky tape to stop it unrolling. I've planted mine in an upside down paper cup with the bottom cut out.

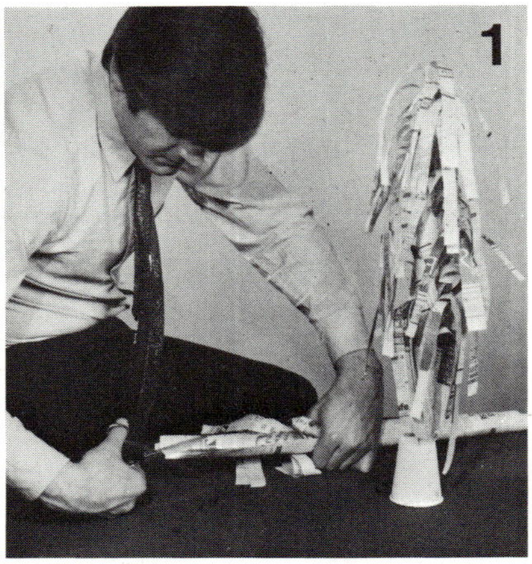

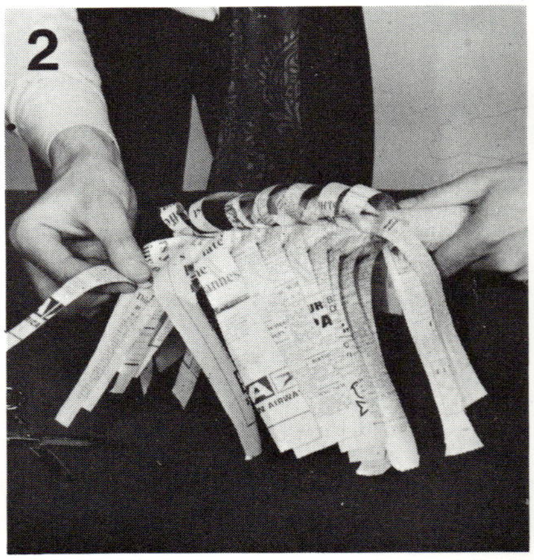

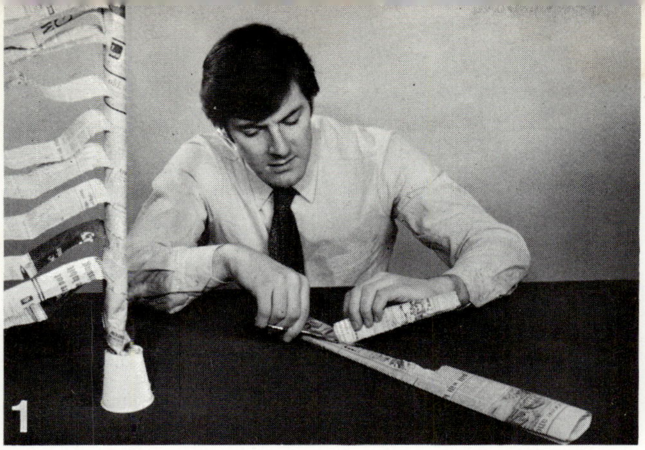

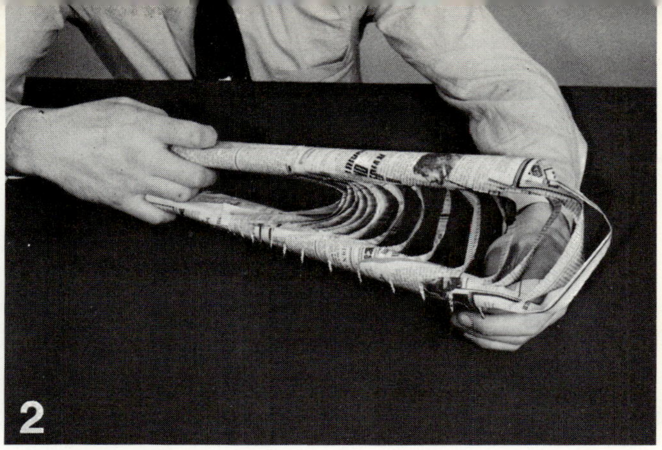

How to make ladders

1 Roll up a sheet of newspaper, flatten it and cut out the centre.
2 Fold the newspaper into a hoop and pull the rungs out gently.

For a really long ladder, roll one sheet of newspaper first and go on adding to the roll by slipping in another sheet and rolling it round the outside of the first one.

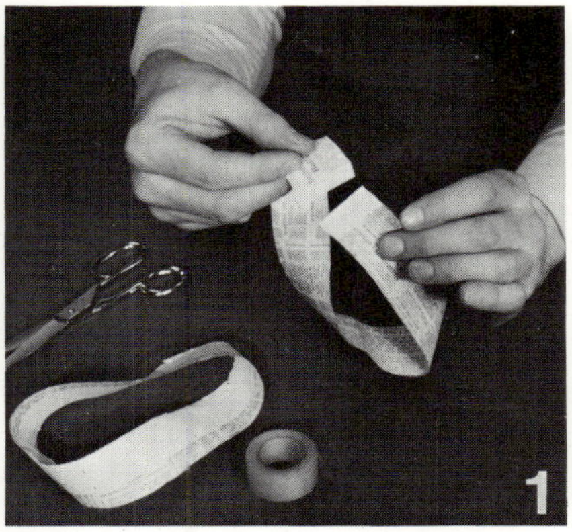

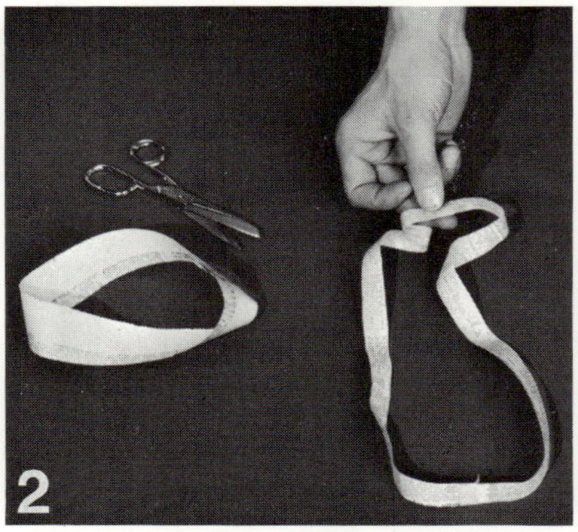

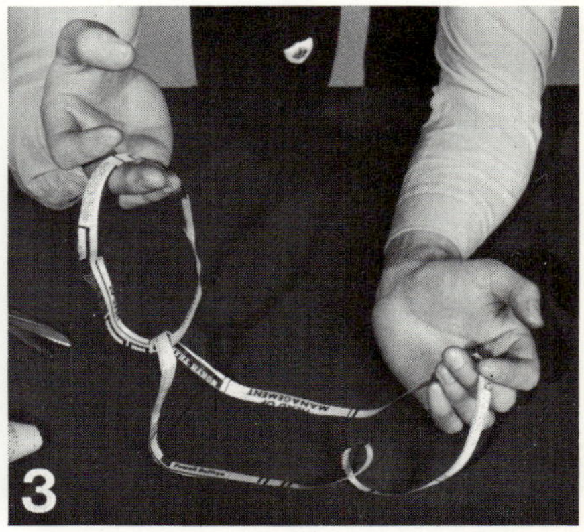

Magic Rings

1 Cut a strip of newspaper, but before you fasten it into a ring make **one** twist in the paper.
Now cut the ring in half right down the middle and . . .

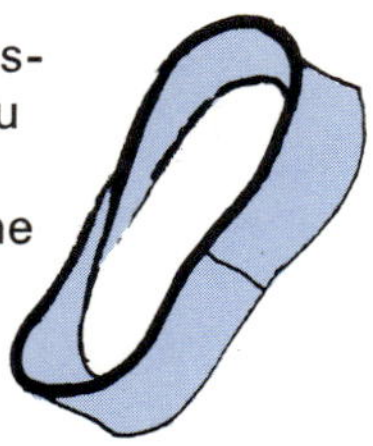

2 this is what happens! Instead of two separate rings you'll get one twice the size!
Now make another ring, but this time,

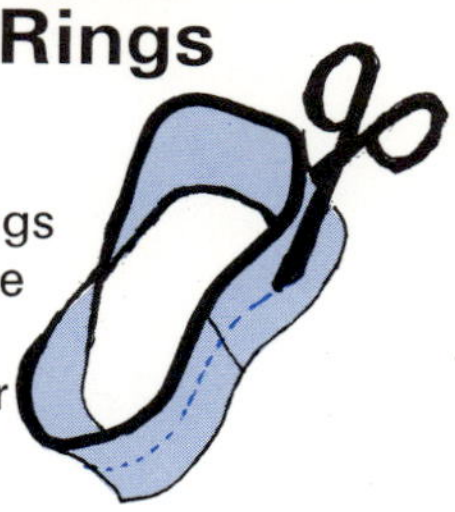

cut the ring a third of its width instead of half and . . .
3 . . . you will get two rings magically linked together.

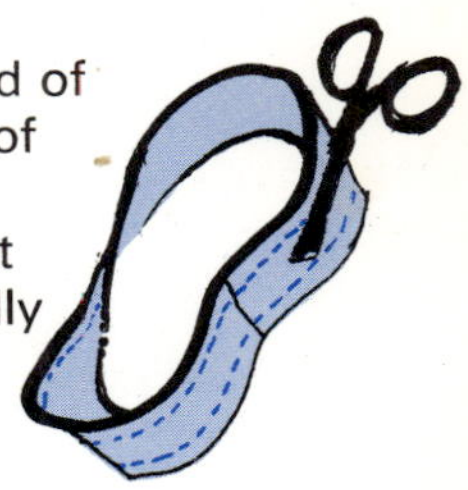

and Impossible Objects

Impossible Triangle

With three equal lengths of wood you can make a triangle. But you can't if you try and join the wood this way! Look carefully and you'll see it's impossible!

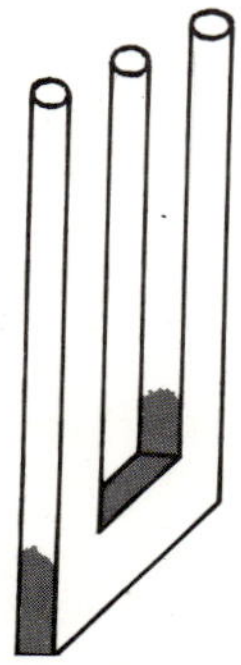

Impossible Cricket Stumps

There are three stumps at the top of this wicket – but just let your eye travel to the bottom. You'll find the middle stump's been knocked out!

The Vanishing Giants

Have *you* seen a steam plough in action?
We had to travel to Amersham in Buckinghamshire to find this one, but a hundred years ago they were a common sight all over Britain – the forerunners of the tractors that farmers use today. Nowadays, you may be lucky enough to spot one in a museum or at a Steam Engine rally, but there are only a handful like this Fowler BB1 that are actually still being used for ploughing.
The idea is that the engines work in pairs, and between them they pull a plough backwards and forwards across a field. The plough is attached by strong wire ropes to revolving cable drums underneath the engines. When the plough reaches the end of the field, the engine that has been pulling it moves forward ready for the return journey. By hauling the plough backwards and forwards across the field, the two engines can plough 20 acres a day, and although this can't compare with modern methods, it's a very good way of cultivating land which has been hardened by the continuous use of tractors.
Weighing at least 20 tons, ploughing engines are tremendously powerful. In the days when they travelled around the countryside in pairs, working for several different farms, one engine would pull a van with living accommodation for the men who operated the machines, whilst the other pulled a tender carrying coal and water.
Although the engines carried about a thousand gallons of water, supplies only lasted for ten miles or so, but it was usually possible to refuel from a convenient pond or stream. The 4 cwt of coal carried would last all day.
Ploughing engines were in general use until the 1920s. Now they've been completely superseded by the modern tractor – but like the old steam trains, there's a magnificence about them that's unforgettable.
The next time there's a rally near where you live – why not go along and see some for yourself!

P S Details of local rallies can be obtained from:-
National Traction Engine Club.
127, Greensted Road, Loughton, Essex.

Basically, a ploughing engine is a traction engine or 'self propelled steam engine'. Water in the boiler **1** is heated and turned into steam by the heat of the fire in the firebox **2**, passing along a series of tubes through the boiler into the smokebox **3**. Steam generated in the boiler passes up to the cylinders **4** where it is made to work by exerting pressure on the pistons **5** and moving them to and fro. A safety valve **6** releases steam if its pressure becomes too great.

The BB1 engine is termed a 'compound' engine, having two cylinders. The smaller of the two receives its steam directly from the boiler and having used it to drive its piston then passes the steam (now at a lower pressure) to the larger cylinder, where it is made to work again, before being allowed to escape through the blast pipe **7** and up the chimney, where it mixes with smoke from the fire.

The back-and-forward motion of the pistons is connected to turn the crankshaft **8**, on one end of which is the big spoked flywheel **9**. The other end is connected to gearwheels **10** which are engaged to drive the shaft to which the driving pinion **11** is fitted, and this is geared to turn one of the large rear driving wheels **12**. These rear wheels are over 6 feet in diameter, with wide rims to lessen the risk of sinking in soft ground.

Around the rims are riveted diagonal strips or 'strakes' to give a good grip on the ground. If the going is really soft (a muddy field for example) then extra strips called 'spuds' **13** can be fitted on the rims. These spuds are normally carried in the spud boxes **14** at the front of the engine. Note that normally only one of the two rear wheels is driven, the other being free to revolve. This makes for easier steering, but should the engine become bogged down in mud then both wheels can be made to drive by locking the far side wheel on its shaft with a steel pin.

The engine is steered by the steering handle **15**, connected by a long shaft to the steering box **16**, which is connected by chains to turn the whole front wheel assembly (called the 'forecarriage').

Slung beneath the boiler is the mechanism used for ploughing — the winding drum **17** on which is wound the strong steel wire rope leading out through a fairlead **18** the end being attached to the plough. The winding drum is driven by a vertical shaft connected by bevel gears **19** to the crankshaft. Fitted on the vertical shaft is a clutch **20** worked by the lever **21** which, when operated causes the top part of the clutch to drop into the bottom half to engage and turn the gear wheel **22**, which in turn revolves the winding drum — to pull the plough towards the engine. When its sister engine is pulling the plough, the clutch is disengaged to allow the drum to revolve freely and the rope to unwind. At the end of each run both engines inch forward to take up position to plough the next furrows — backwards and forwards goes the plough until the whole field is ploughed.

As the drivers of the two engines have to keep in touch with each other, a pre-arranged system of signals is sounded out on each engine's whistle **23**.

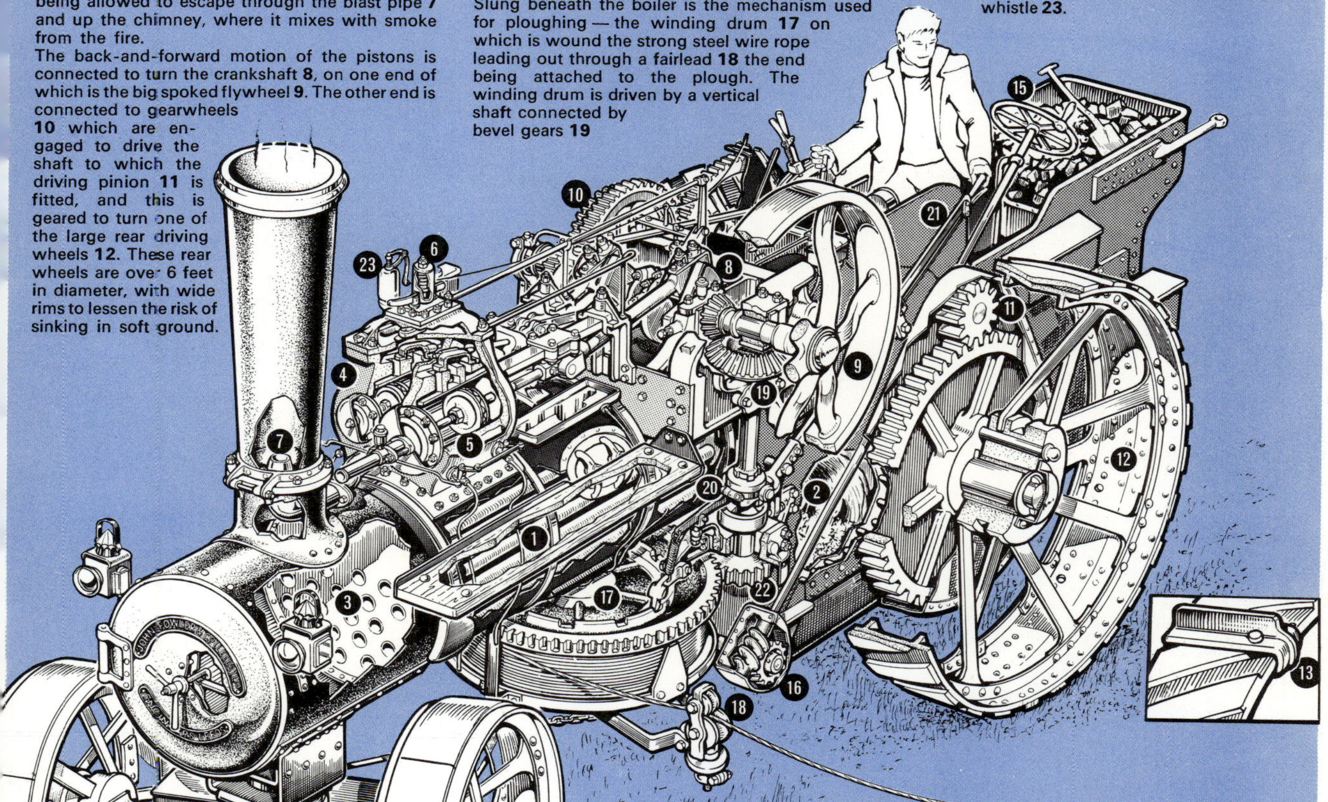

A large 10-furrow 'anti-balance' held on a straight course by a steersman. One set of ploughshares is held aloft while the others are in use. For its return run, the plough is toppled like a see-saw and the steersman changes ends.

Inside the Fowler BB1

Success for Cindy

Do you remember when Cindy first joined 'Blue Peter'? She was only five weeks old – but we hoped that one day she would be as successful as her half sister, Honey – our first 'Blue Peter' Guide Dog for the Blind.

Cindy began her success story after we'd looked after her for a year. Puppy Walking Manager, Derek Freeman, gave her an extensive test – he took her on trains, buses, into crowded supermarkets, past deafening pneumatic drills, and even into church!

We kept our fingers crossed! We knew Cindy was good at things like walking up and down hazardous flights of steps, and that she was totally unafraid of crowds, but if anything, she was a little *too* friendly. With one enthusiastic leap towards someone or something she liked, she could easily pull you across half the pavement – not the sort of behaviour expected from a reliable trainee Guide Dog.

One year old—Cindy's first day at Training School outside her special centrally heated kennel.

Five weeks old—Cindy's first day on 'Blue Peter'.

Then –

'Congratulations!' said Derek, 'you've done a grand job – Cindy's well up to standard – I'd like her to join the Training Centre as soon as possible.'

We felt glad and sorry at the same time. It was sad to part with Cindy – but we knew she could only pass her other tests by going away for her advanced training. Still, Honey had been very happy at Leamington, and we knew Cindy would be in good hands.

On February 13th, 1969, I took Cindy to Leamington. She seemed to feel at home right from the start – and even wagged her tail as I handed her over to Derek.

Ever since, we've had splendid progress bulletins. Cindy's gone from strength to strength.

We feel very proud of her success – and proud of *you*, too. After all, if it hadn't been for all your silver paper and milk bottle tops, we'd never have been able to have two 'Blue Peter' Guide Dogs for the Blind!

The Little Musician

1 In the heart of Austria lies the town of Salzburg with its magnificent castles and palaces, but the most famous building of all is

2 a little house in a quiet square where the Mozart family lived. Two centuries ago, in a tiny flat on the third floor

3 a baby was born. He was called Wolfgang Amadeus Mozart, and as he lay in his cradle he heard music.

4 His father, Leopold Mozart, was a court musician and played the violin. His sister, Nanerl, was learning the clavier although she was only five years old.

5 One day when Wolfgang was three, he watched, fascinated, as Nanerl's fingers flew over the keys. Then

6 he climbed on to the stool and played the tune himself! He played perfectly, made no mistakes, and he'd never had a lesson.

7 Young Wolfgang was a genius. Now his father taught him everything he knew and Wolfgang's talent grew and grew.

8 Three years later, Leopold Mozart set off with Wolfgang and Nanerl to see the world and show them off to important people. They were to visit England, France and Italy, but

9 first they went to Vienna, where the two young children were invited to play at the Palace of Schonbrunn before the Empress of Austria.

10 Inside the palace they gave a concert for the Empress Maria Theresa and her court. Dressed in fine clothes they looked very grand and played their very best. That night

11 a messenger came to their lodging. He brought a purse of gold from the Empress, a court dress of pink and silver for Nanerl and a courtier's suit of lilac and gold for Wolfgang.

12 He had his portrait painted wearing this suit and he looked so stiff and formal he could hardly recognise himself.

13 Next they went to Versailles, the greatest palace in the world, and played before the King and Queen of France. Afterwards they were allowed to

14 stand and watch while the King and Queen ate their dinner. This was considered a great honour and

15 the Queen fed Wolfgang with tit-bits from her plate—just as though he were a little dog!

16 At last Wolfgang came home. Now he began to write down the music he could hear so clearly in his head. But as he grew up, people lost interest in him. He went to

17 Vienna, the city that he loved the most. Here he'd had his first success, and here he lived and worked until he died. Wolfgang never found fortune, but he did find fame. To this day his beautiful music is loved by millions of people all over the world.

It wasn't really you was it?

That's what a bunch of boys asked me when I was signing their autograph books outside Tottenham football ground. They'd watched 'Blue Peter' on Monday and seen me dressed as a musketeer fighting for my life against no less than five swordsmen on the ramparts of Hever Castle.

1 Derek's 'cavaliers' rehearsing for their latest epic.

2 Derek showed me the basic attacks for a 'give and take' routine.

3 Every cut and thrust in a filmed fight is carefully planned and rehearsed.

4 This is how to parry a cut to the cheek.

I had gone there to meet Derek Ware, and some of his 'cavaliers', to find out how an epic sword fight for the screen is made.

Duelling for the stage or for films is very different from competition fencing. Derek explained this to me as I watched four of his men going at it hammer and tongs practising for the latest B.B.C. costume drama.

'Every move those boys are making has been planned as carefully as the steps in a ballet. In competition fencing you obviously don't know what the other fellow's going to do next. But in an arranged film fight, you must know every thrust and parry, while still giving the impression that you're fighting to the death.'

I asked Derek how long it took to train one of his duellists.

'It takes quite a time to become really good like these boys,' he said. 'But I reckon I could teach you a simple routine in a morning.'

Derek tossed me a sabre and said –

'Right – there are five basic attacks. Flank – cheek – other cheek – head – and other flank.'

On each word Derek thrust his sword at the appropriate part of my body, and I automatically put up *my* sword to fend off each movement.

'That's good – what you were doing then is called a parry.'

'So we do that only faster?' I asked.

'No, no, no. It's no good just standing up there clouting each other's blades. We've got to arrange a "give and take" routine.'

Derek raised his sword and began to fight in slow motion.

'I cut to your cheek – you parry – now push my blade away slightly and go for my head – good. Now I'm going for your other cheek – parry! And lunge at my head again. One, two, three and four – good! Now this time thrust at me – yes – and hold it!'

Derek showed me how to turn the blade when making a thrust so that the blade bent instead of pushing into the opponent. Exactly the opposite to fighting a real duel!

'Right – we'll do it again, only a little faster – and this time go for me and not my sword. Go!'

We battled on throughout the morning. Derek is a perfectionist. The fight must look lethal and still be a hundred per cent safe. And this can only be achieved by practice – practice – and more practice.

5 We all changed into costume and the 'Blue Peter' cameras began to film 'The Escape from Hever Castle'.

6 I was up on the battlements in mortal combat with one of my captors.

7 My opponent bit the dust – but a second swordsman barred my way.

8 The moment my back was turned, a third appeared, and the next instant . . .

At last Derek was satisfied, and after lunch we went off to be made up and fitted for our costumes.

By 2.30 p.m. everything was ready, and the 'Blue Peter' cameras began to film the drama of 'The Escape from Hever Castle.'

I was up on the battlements in mortal combat with one of my captors.

'One, two – cheek – parry – head and thrust!'

With a blood-curdling scream my opponent bit the dust. But as I turned, another swordsman barred my way. Down the stone steps we fought; at one moment he had me pinned against the wall – the point of his blade at my throat. I placed my foot square on his chest and pushed. One, two, three and thrust. Ahhh! I leapt over his lifeless body and out into the courtyard. There was only the drawbridge now between me and freedom.

I looked cautiously around – and then from out of the shadows came not one, but five gleaming swords. I was surrounded!

One by one they came – then two and three together. The odds seemed impossible. But looking down from the ramparts the 'Blue Peter' cameras saw me slay all five with a single blow!

The portcullis was up – and I, like a bird, flew across the courtyard towards freedom. But from behind a pillar came two *more* swordsmen to bar my way. I had the first in no time – but the second came at me from behind and as I turned, I slipped and fell to the ground. 'Portcullis!' he yelled. And the great spiked gate began to thunder down on my helpless body. I kicked out at my assailant's feet and brought him down beside me. There we grappled whilst the murderous spikes of the portcullis loomed nearer and nearer. With less than a foot to go I broke his vice-like grip and rolled clear as the great gate gored his prostrate body.

Only the drawbridge to cross and I was free.

'Have at you – now!' rang out a voice.

I turned to see two more guards advancing across the drawbridge. The first came on at the run – I side-stepped quickly, and he plunged into the icy waters of the moat. Now only one swordsman remained – and soon I had him pinned against the side of the drawbridge. His free hand flew to his belt and in a flash he had a dagger at my throat. It was a trial of strength. The first one to lose his grip was a dead man. I summoned up all the strength in my body. At last he gave a little groan of surrender and then toppled backwards to join his friend in the moat.

I was free. I had fought my way out of Hever Castle against impossible odds. Nobody could touch me now.

There was a rustle in the undergrowth. A cavalier who, to my certain knowledge, I had already killed three times, was barring my way to escape.

9 . . . I was surrounded. How could I possibly escape?

10 Above the high ramparts, the cameras watched me fight my way to freedom.

'It depends on who's arranging the fight,' he said. 'One, two, three and thrust.'
Ahhhhh.
I died like a hero as the sun went down behind the castle.
'Cut,' called the film director.
I got up and took off my false beard. 'The Escape from Hever Castle' was over.

'Well done, Peter,' smiled Derek. 'You nearly got away with it. You see, you can take on a whole army – provided the fight arranger is on your side!'
Film duelling was certainly far more complex and demanding than I'd ever imagined, and the next time I see swordsmen in action in the cinema or on TV, I'll think of all the skill and planning that goes into making a first-class fight.

11 The portcullis thundered down on my helpless body.

12 I broke away just in time – but my assailant was not fast enough.

13 Two men barred the drawbridge . . .

14 Now only one swordsman stood between me and freedom.

15 For certain victory you only need one ally – the man who arranges the fights.

APPEAL

'Dear Blue Peter,

Who's idea was it to have an appeal for West Africa?

Aren't there enough good causes in England?'

This was the rather unpleasant letter that arrived in the 'Blue Peter' office the day after we launched our appeal. True, there were 5,000 letters saying what a super idea it was – but we do sometimes get nasty letters like that. Happily, in this case, there was a very straight and simple answer – the idea was YOURS! Because 'Blue Peter' viewers do seem to care about what's happening to other people. All through the summer, letters kept pouring in saying,

'What can we do to help the victims of that terrible war in West Africa?'

It wasn't easy to find an answer – because the problem of two million starving people, with numbers growing every day, is so enormous that it makes you feel like giving up before you start. We took advice from a relief organisation which has teams working in the front line, and they said:—

'You can't do better than send them a Hospital Truck. Things are changing all the time, but right now, they need a Hospital Truck.'

A Hospital Truck is a hospital actually built into a long wheel based land-rover. Outside, it's an ordinary, tough, four wheel drive truck – like the one that took us bumping through Morocco on our Safari. But inside, it's like a fully equipped hospital, with a mobile operating theatre, stainless steel sink unit, refrigerator, telescopic stretcher, drugs, medicines and all the surgical equipment necessary for emergency treatment.

That was what was needed.

The question was – how?

'What about stamps again?' asked John.

'No – people are still sending stamps for the "Blue Peter" House for the homeless from last year,' Val reminded us. 'It would be too confusing.'

'The same goes for paper backed books and lifeboats,' put in Peter.

'And silver paper and guide dogs,' added Val.

'We haven't asked for wool for ages,' said John.

Peter raised his eyebrows.

'Have you any idea how much wool we'd need?'

'No,' John replied. 'But you're good at sums – you go away and work it out!'

Two minutes later Peter was back with the answer.

'If everybody puts one tatty sweater, an old scarf and a pair of rotten socks in a parcel, it would take 144,000 parcels to buy our truck.'
We all thought it was an enormous target – but because 'Blue Peter' hadn't let us down yet, we decided to have a go. We were right to be optimistic. But we didn't know quite how right we were going to be proved.
By Christmas we were well past our target of 144,000 parcels – but the wool was still pouring in! We'd already filled a Church – two Drill Halls – and a gigantic warehouse!
On January 2nd, we announced the result of the Appeal. Not 144,000 parcels – but one million, four hundred thousand – ten times what we'd asked for!
When all that wool was sold, it was worth over £20,000. Enough to buy *two* hospital trucks and six Emergency Doctor's Cars – fast Estate cars specially designed to take teams of doctors, nurses and nutritional experts into the emergency areas. As well as this, there were some special jet injectors which could inoculate people at the rate of 600 an hour.
Altogether, the Hospital Trucks and the Emergency Doctor's Cars, together with the jet injectors, cost £11,200. The remaining £8,800 was to go on drugs and medicines, and to help pay for the air-lift to get aid to the stricken areas.
Just for the record, this is the result of 'Blue Peter' appeals over the past five years:

Appeal	Target	Result
1964 1 guide dog for the blind	3 tons of silver paper	$7\frac{1}{2}$ tons of silver paper=$2\frac{1}{2}$ guide dogs (Honey, Cindy—£125 over)
1965 A tractor for the Busoga arm School, Africa	15,000 parcels of wool	45,000 parcels=1 tractor, 1 disc plough, 1 rotavator, 1 rigger. Plus fuel & maintenance for 1 year
1966 1 Inshore rescue boat	60,000 paper backed books	240,000 paper backed books=4 inshore rescue boats
1967 1 house converted into 2 flats to house two homeless families	120,000,000 used stamps	360,000,000 stamps=3 houses making flats for six families
1968 1 hospital truck for West Africa	144,000 parcels of wool	1,400,000 parcels=2 hospital trucks, 6 emergency doctor's cars, jet injectors plus £8,800 to be spent on vital drugs & air-lift to the stricken areas

A Star Danced
The Story of Anna Pavlova

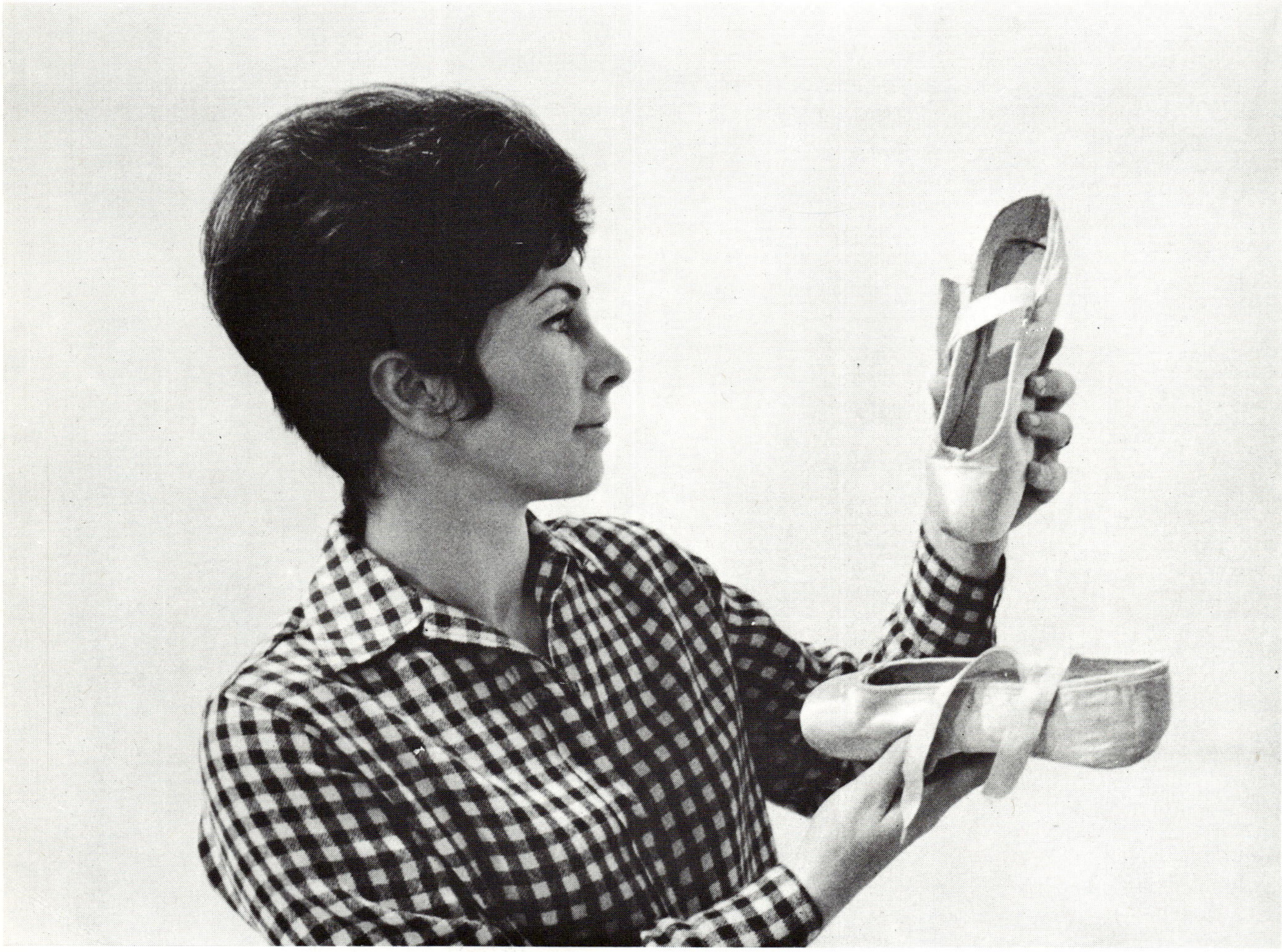

These shoes I am holding belonged to the most famous ballerina in the world – this is her story...

The snow lay deep in the wintry streets of St Petersburg. The street lamps shone like stars, and sleighs ran smoothly, drawn by trotting horses with jingling bells, their passengers wrapped up in heavy rugs.

In one sleigh, a little girl looked out in wild excitement, trying to force the horses to move more quickly.

'Faster, faster,' she murmured.

She was eight years old, and she was going to the theatre for the first time, for a special Christmas treat, to see the ballet. Her name was Anna Pavlova.

Her father was dead, and her mother was very poor. She had no brothers or sisters, so they lived very quietly, though always there were presents and treats at holidays – an Easter egg full of toys, a Christmas tree with candles and golden fruit.

Now this was the biggest treat of all – a visit to the Marinsky Theatre of St Petersburg, to see the

Imperial Russian Ballet dance *The Sleeping Beauty*.

At last they had arrived. The theatre lay just ahead, and Anna's mother turned to her. 'You are going to enter fairyland,' she told her.

When the curtain went up, showing the dazzling forms of the dancers in the enchanted castle, whirling and turning to the tuneful beautiful music, Anna believed her – this was a magic world!

She made up her mind at that very moment – this was going to be *her* world!

Her mother sensed her excitement. 'Wouldn't you like to join the people on the stage and dance with them?' she asked.

'Oh no,' said Anna, '*I* would rather dance on my own, like the Sleeping Beauty. And one day I will – in this very theatre!'

Imperial Ballet School. He smiled at the thin eager little girl. 'We can't take eight year olds,' he said. 'Bring her back when she is ten – if she still wants to come!'

The next two years passed very slowly for Anna, with her dreams of becoming a great dancer.

But at last it was her tenth birthday. She begged her mother to take her back to the Director. Her mother looked sad, but she kept her promise.

Anna was given a rigorous medical check-up, and tests for intelligence and gracefulness, and at last she was accepted by the Ballet School attached to the Marinsky Theatre. Here boys and girls were taught to dance, and studied the history of dancing, and given a general education, until they were 16 years old. Then they entered the corps de ballet of the

Anna joined the Imperial Ballet School when she was ten years old.

At 18 she was a member of the corps de ballet at the Marinsky Theatre.

25 and a Prima Ballerina of the Russian Ballet.

Eight-year old Anna Pavlova had decided – she would be a great dancer. And never for a single moment all her life did she change her mind, or regret the choice she had made.

Next day, back home after the great visit to the theatre, Anna pleaded with her mother. 'You will have me taught to dance, won't you?'

Her mother explained. 'You would have to leave home, and become a pupil at the Ballet School and live there all the time. You wouldn't like that, would you?'

Anna was quite firm. 'Of course I don't want to go away from you. But if that is the only way to become a dancer, I shall have to.'

So her mother took her to see the Director of the

Marinsky Theatre, and after a while they were promoted to be solo dancers. The best of all were given the title of Prima Ballerina, and they danced the great star parts – the Sleeping Princess, Giselle, Odette in *Swan Lake*. It was a long road after joining the Ballet School, with hard work and fierce determination needed for every step of the way.

At school, Anna wore the school uniform, a dark blue dress, with a little white apron and cape, with her hair drawn back from her face. On Sundays she saw her mother, and told her about her classes. Soon her reports called her 'capable' and 'very attentive', and her teachers were expecting great things from her.

Anna was worried because she was rather tall and

very thin and she swallowed bottles of cod-liver oil to try to get fatter. But soon critics saw the charm of her fragile air, and her pointed face with huge dark eyes – she was to set a new standard of beauty in a dancer.

At last her training was finished, and she appeared on the stage of the Marinsky Theatre. Very soon she was picked out from the corps de ballet to dance small parts, and she developed as a skilful and beautiful dancer. In 1906, when she was 25, Anna Pavlova was made a prima ballerina of the Russian Ballet. A great career lay before her.

She loved dancing, and it was her whole life. She practised for hours every day, to become more perfect, and she wanted to share her joy of dancing with more people. Outside Russia, ballet was almost unkown. Anna Pavlova began to make visits to other cities in Europe, dancing before new audiences, who became fascinated by the magic world that was new to them.

Once in Sweden after a performance, crowds followed her back to her hotel, blocking the street and cheering and clapping until she appeared on her balcony. She was very moved by all this, and she said to her maid 'What have I done, to make them so enthusiastic?'

'Madam,' said the girl. 'You have made them happy by making them forget for an hour the sadness of their lives.'

Her words were a revelation to Anna Pavlova – it gave her a new ideal of what her dancing could mean. She was determined to take it to as many people as possible.

And this is what she did, forming her own ballet company, and spending the rest of her life taking it all round the world. Most of her audiences had never seen ballet before. She showed it to them and made them love it. The tremendous interest in ballet in so many countries today comes from the excitement that Pavlova inspired by her dancing.

Visiting Egypt in 1922 – the Pavlova ballet company danced in countries all over the world.

The Swan – Anna Pavlova's greatest role.

One ballet she danced so often that it is always thought of as her special dance. It was called The Swan: in it she appeared as a lovely graceful swan, drifting to music, gradually becoming weaker, fluttering and trying to soar again to flight, but at last falling back dead. Although it was so sad, the beauty and grace of The Swan made it everyone's favourite.

When she died, she had travelled hundreds of thousands of miles, and danced to people in every part of the world. She had given them all something rare and beautiful.

And for thousands of girls, to be taken as a special treat to see Anna Pavlova dance, was something they would remember all their lives – just as Anna Pavlova herself never forgot her first glimpse of ballet, at the Marinsky Theatre when she was eight years old.

This is the toughest thing I've ever done on Blue Peter

You wouldn't believe it would you? But it's true

When you work on 'Blue Peter' you need to keep pretty fit. You never know when the phone will ring and a familiar voice at the other end will say: 'We're doing the Army's toughest assault course today, John.'
or (on a very cold day last March)
' . . . you'll be picked up out of the sea by a power boat travelling at 15 knots.'

These things you have to take in your stride; so when they said:
'Meet you at the Royal Ballet School in Richmond Park,' I said to myself, 'Noakes – today will be a pushover!' The next day I felt so stiff, I thought I'd never walk again.

White Lodge is a super place to have a school. Standing right in the middle of Richmond Park, it's just like being in the countryside – and yet it only takes 45 minutes to get to the Royal Opera House, Covent Garden, in the heart of London.

Getting to the Royal Opera House, Covent Garden, is the ambition of most of the pupils I met at White Lodge. But by 'getting there' they mean joining the Royal Ballet Company, and that takes about eight years. Boys *and* girls go to the Royal Ballet School, and they start at the age of 11 or 12.

The School can only take about 35 new pupils a year, so, as you can imagine, the competition for places is pretty fierce.

Although you needn't have had any dancing experience, you *will* have to pass a pretty stiff audition to find out if you have it in you to be a dancer. After that you're given a very thorough medical examina-

1 'Tail in – stomach in – head up – toes out – out – *out!*'

2 A grand jeté seemed a bit easier . . .

3. . . but my landing appeared to lack finesse.

tion to make sure you're strong enough, followed by a *school* examination to see if you're clever enough. If you pass all these tests, you'll be whirled off to another doctor who'll decide how tall you're going to be when you grow up. After all, the Royal Ballet would look pretty peculiar in ten years time if all the girls were 6′ tall, and all the boys were 4′ 6″.

You don't get out of 'ordinary school' at White Lodge. As well as ballet and music, all the normal grammar school subjects are taught to 'O' level standard. At the age of 16, the pupils move to the Upper School, which is nearer the centre of London (and closer still to Covent Garden!) Here they have a final two-year course with the emphasis very strongly on ballet.

Every ballet dancer in the world from Margot Fonteyn downwards goes to a daily class. This is because ballet is so demanding that if you didn't keep your muscles in the peak of condition, you'd never get through a performance.

If Nureyev had to go to class, why not Noakes – so I took my place at the bar with the Junior ballet class. Every class begins with bar work.

'Et 5th position – degagé – et stretch – et derrière – et head up – à la seconde –'
the piano tinkled away as Walter Trevor, the ballet master, rapped out instructions firmly, rhythmically, and in a mixture of French and English.

All the basic positions in ballet have French names, because ballet began in the court of Louis XIV, the King of France. It seems at first like an unnecessary complication; but once you've learnt it, you can travel anywhere in the world, and still be able to understand the ballet master.

My basic problem was my stance –
'tail in – stomach in – head up – et à la seconde – toes out – out! – *out*!'

As he spoke, Walter kicked my feet until they were

4 They all came down as I went up – somebody must have got it wrong!

5 Next door the girls' class was in full swing.

6 A girl standing on one leg – leaning forward on your outstretched arm – can get to be a problem.

7 Et lift – Hold her! – *Hold!*

in a complete quarter to three position.

'Head up! – up! – *up*! Et plié –'

This meant he wanted me to bend both knees – keep my back straight – and my head up, with my feet still pointing in opposite directions!

Well – you try it! Anybody who thinks ballet is for cissies must be out of his mind.

A dancer is an athlete who's an artiste as well. He's got to be just as tough as a four-minute miler, but with one big difference. A dancer can't collapse when he passes the winning post. He must never appear to be making the slightest effort, even when he feels his lungs are about to burst with exhaustion.

As well as all the fireworks of jumping and turning in the air, the male dancer must be a perfect support for his partner.

For this he needs style, precision, strength and nerve. I seemed to lack all of these except, I suppose, I did have the nerve to ask Rashna Homji from the Upper School if she'd let me be her support for one short pas de deux.

'One and two and lunge – strong arm the boys – *strong*!'

Rashna wasn't very heavy, but a girl standing on one leg, leaning forward onto your outstretched arm, can become a problem.

I felt my arm wobbling with the effort – and Rashna's nose was getting nearer and nearer the floor.

'*Still* John – *hold* her!'

The music stopped just in time to avoid disaster.

'Et reste'

'Et four petits changements and a grand changement. 5th position – right foot devant – et – '

The piano started again – faster this time.

'Et lift – hold her! – *Hold*!'

I grabbed Rashna firmly round the waist and lifted as she jumped – and she soared above me as light as a feather.

'Good John. Et reste.'

At last I'd got something right! For one fleeting moment I felt I knew what it was like to be a ballet dancer, although I don't think Rudolph Nureyev needs to worry – just yet!

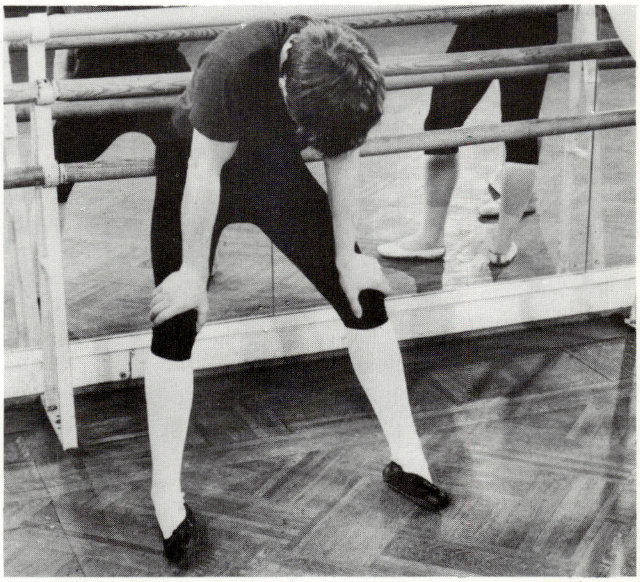

8 Anybody who says ballet dancing is for cissies must be out of his mind.

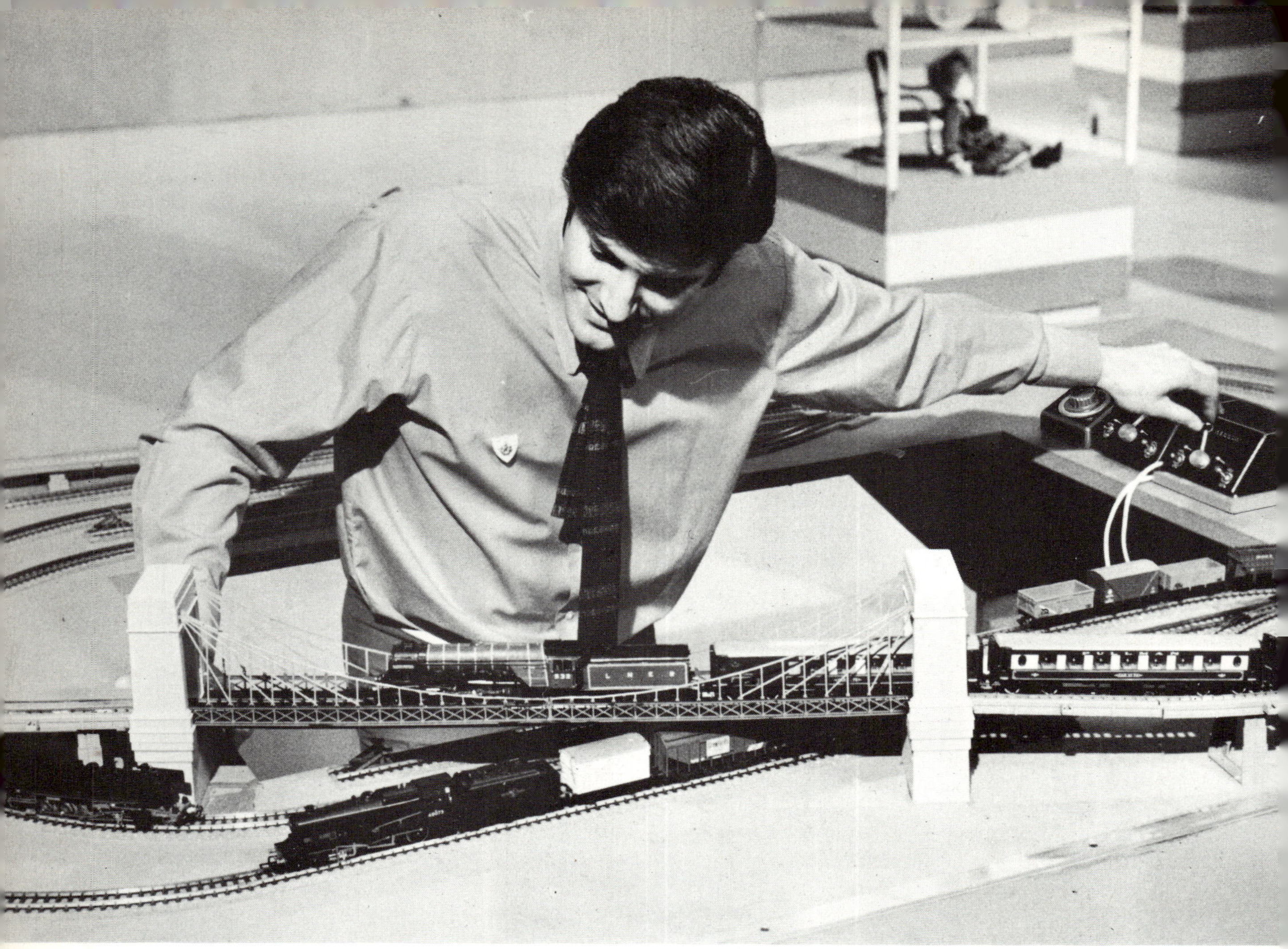

Blue Peter Layout

Disaster! Freight train smashes into Express! Famous Loco 532 Blue Peter derailed on bridge!

That accident hasn't happened yet, but if I made a mistake when I was showing trains on the programme, it just might! That's why our 'Blue Peter' layout has a hole in the middle. It's been specially designed so that I can reach every part of the track without having to move. I can get the express back on the rails without getting in front of the cameras and blocking your view. As well as being easy to operate, the layout is very compact.

The base board measures 8 feet by 5 feet and that includes 4 feet by 2 feet of hole! Even so, I've managed to fit in just about thirty-five yards of track. It's an 00 gauge two rail system that runs off 12 volt controllers. The trains on the inner and outer loops can be run independently. To get the most variety out of a small layout, I've put in an overhead section and a turntable. In the sketch plan you can see how I've fitted everything in.

The suspension bridge on the overhead section is just over 2′ 6″ long. The loco on the bridge is my old 60532 which I've repainted in LNER livery and renumbered 532 just like the real Blue Peter.

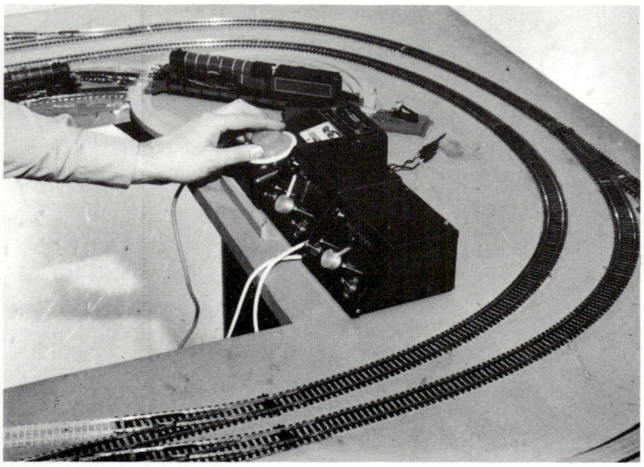

I use two special controllers so that I can run the trains at scale speed. By using these I can run the heavy goods trains like the 2 - 8 - 0 at a model scale speed of 30 mph and the diesel expresses at 80 mph. The third controller is for the turntable.

The turntable is like the ones you used to see at British rail terminal stations. In the sketch plan you can see how I can direct a loco in to either of two tracks.

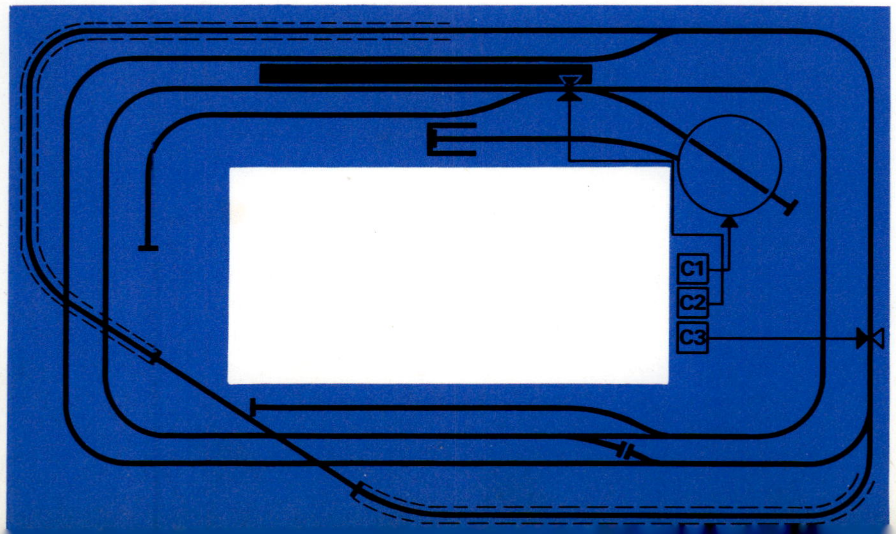

Sketch Plan of
Blue Peter Layout

C1 controller

feed points

embankment to bridge

insulated section

Paddington Goes Halves

A Story by Michael Bond. Illustrated by 'Hargreaves'

'Has anyone seen the paper serviettes?' Mrs. Brown looked up hopefully from the sideboard cupboard. 'It's very strange. I put a new packet here only this afternoon. Now they've gone.'

'Perhaps it's the Phantom Paper Snatcher of Notting Hill Gate,' said Jonathan, glancing up from his homework. 'Someone's pinched my best graph paper as well.'

'That's funny,' broke in Judy. 'I'm sure my drawing book used to be thicker.'

Mrs. Bird rose from behind the wastepaper basket. 'If it *is* the Phantom Paper Snatcher,' she said, 'you might ask him what he's done with my shopping list. It's completely disappeared!'

The others exchanged mystified glances and a buzz of conversation broke out in the dining-room of number thirty-two Windsor Gardens as they began to piece together the strange jig-saw puzzle of missing items.

Mr. Brown looked up from his newspaper. 'I do wish you wouldn't make so much noise,' he grumbled. 'Anyone would think the world was about to come to an end. All this fuss about a few scraps of paper. I . . . ' Mr. Brown broke off suddenly as he turned a page, 'Who's taken my sports section?' he demanded. 'Come on, own up. Who's taken it?'

'I suppose it's a different story now?' said Mrs. Brown meaningly.

'We can do without serviettes,' snorted Mr. Brown. 'This is a serious matter. I wanted to read about the golf tournament.'

'Who would do it?' he asked, looking round the room, '*Who* would possibly do a thing like that?'

'Oh crumbs!' Jonathan and Judy looked at each other.

'Quick!' said Jonathan. 'Follow me.'

As the Browns hurried up the stairs they none of them knew quite what to expect, but the sight which greeted their eyes as Jonathan flung open one of the landing doors drew a gasp of astonishment.

For, to say the least, the room beyond was in a state.

There was paper everywhere. Paper of all shapes, sizes and conditions. It covered the bed, the dressing table, the window sill, the chair, and even overflowed on to the floor, where it lay in great piles and mounds like a set-piece for the Desert Song.

In the middle of it all, clutching a pair of scissors in one paw and what looked like a half-finished boat in the other, sat a familiar brown figure.

'Paddington' cried Mrs. Brown. 'What on earth's going on? I've never seen such a mess!'

'A *mess*, Mrs. Brown?' exclaimed Paddington, looking most offended. 'It's not a mess. It's only my entry!'

'Your *entry*?' repeated Mr. Brown. He gazed at the object in Paddington's paw with a marked lack of enthusiasm. Clearly visible on one of the sails was a picture of a man carrying a golf club. 'What entry?'

'I'm going in for a Blue Peter competition,' Paddington announced importantly, blissfully unaware of the effect he was having. 'I'm afraid I'm having trouble with my Origami!'

* * * *

'Well,' remarked Mrs. Brown, later that evening, 'We must be thankful for one thing. At least it hasn't got anything to do with glue. Paper folding may be untidy but it's clean.'

'It doesn't even have to be paper,' said Judy. 'I watched the programme and Val said you can use anything.'

'It tells you all about it here,' broke in Jonathan. He picked up a copy of the *Radio Times* which was lying open at the 'Blue Peter Postbag' page. 'They're giving three prizes. One for the best idea, one for the best model, and one for the most original material. It sounds jolly good.'

'Mmm,' said Mrs. Bird ominously. 'That's as maybe, but what's good for some people isn't always good for others.'

The Browns' housekeeper spoke from long experience of keeping Paddington supplied with used soap cartons and old yoghurt pots, for Paddington was a keen Blue Peter fan and some evenings after Valerie's demonstrations he remained 'glued' to the television receiver in more ways than one, long after the programme finished.

But for once her worst fears seemed to go unrealised, and despite the large number of half-finished models which began to appear in cupboards, heavily marked with labels like TOP SEACRET, she found little to grumble at during the days that followed.

Indeed, as time went by even Mrs. Bird began to be infected by the excitement and twice she arrived home carrying a large roll of paper, while Paddington himself paid several visits to the nearby market in order to consult his friend, Mr. Gruber, on the subject.

Apart from keeping an antique shop, Mr. Gruber also specialised in old books and he lent Paddington a volume entitled 'A THOUSAND AND ONE THINGS YOU CAN DO WITH A SHEET OF PAPER.'

According to the author, Mr. Ivor Fold, if you armed yourself with but a single sheet of paper the world was your oyster and to prove his point the first illustration in the book showed him prising open a large model of one in order to remove a pearl.

Paddington sat up in bed for several nights carefully reading the instructions and he nearly frightened Mrs. Bird to death some days later when he emerged from his room carrying the result of his efforts.

Far from looking like an oyster, Paddington's model was more of a cross between an octopus and a giant marrow and when he squeezed it, instead of a pearl, the half-eaten remains of a marmalade sandwich fell out.

'I hope he doesn't try sending *that* through the post,' said Mrs. Brown as he disappeared down the garden. 'He'll have them all out on strike.'

But Paddington had other things on his mind. With the closing date of the competition drawing near a feeling of panic was beginning to come over him and as he settled himself down behind the raspberry canes with a jar of his favourite marmalade in one paw and Mr. Fold's book in the other, he wore a very worried expression indeed.

The models in the book grew larger and more complicated as page succeeded page, and on the end-piece Mr. Fold himself was shown climbing into an enormous space rocket made entirely of paper, as he waved goodbye to his readers.

Paddington had had his eye on this particular model ever since Mr. Gruber had given him the book and for the next few minutes, apart from the sound of heavy breathing and an occasional crumpling noise, all was quiet.

Mr. Fold's paper was always shown neatly laid out on a table with never a mark on it, whereas looking at his own piece Paddington had to admit that it was in a bit of a mess, with earth, cabbage leaves, marmalade stains and goodness knows what else covering the surface. Apart from that, every time he unrolled it in one direction the other end followed on behind. And when he did finally manage to stand up he found himself firmly encased in a long tube, utterly unable to give any kind of wave, let alone a farewell one.

It was while he was struggling to release himself that he suddenly heard his name being called and he realised with a sinking heart that the Browns' neighbour, Mr. Curry, was addressing him.

Mr. Curry had a reputation in the neighbourhood for being bad-tempered at the best of times and by the sound of his voice it certainly wasn't one of those.

'Bear!' roared Mr. Curry. 'What's going on, bear?'

Paddington took a deep breath. 'It's alright, Mr. Curry,' he called in muffled tones. 'I'm only having trouble with a join in my *Origami*.'

'Go and join the army?' repeated Mr. Curry. 'How dare you bear!' he spluttered. 'I shall have to report you for this, I . . .'

'Not *join the army*, Mr. Curry,' cried Paddington desperately. '*Origami*. It's a *rocket*. I've got to finish it *today*.'

'*Stop it!*' bellowed Mr. Curry. '*Go away!* I most certainly will do no such thing.'

Paddington struggled to his feet and peered out from the top of the tube. 'Oh no, Mr. Curry,' he said anxiously. 'I didn't say *go away*. I wouldn't say that even though I wish you would, I mean . . . ' Paddington's voice died away as he caught sight of the Browns' neighbour glaring over the top of the fence.

'I'll have you know, bear, you've ruined my afternoon's sleep,' barked Mr. Curry. 'I demand an explanation.'

'Oh, I've got one of those, Mr. Curry,' said Paddington, hastily launching into a long account of his activities.

Mr. Curry's normally grim expression began to relax as he listened to the tale and when Paddington had finished he eyed the rocket thoughtfully.

'You say there's a prize for the best model?' he asked casually.

Paddington nodded. 'I don't suppose I shall win one though, Mr. Curry,' he said sadly, as he clambered out of his rocket and surveyed the battered remains. 'Tomorrow's the closing date for the entries and I haven't anything left to make mine with.'

A crafty expression came over Mr. Curry's face. 'How would it be if *I* let you have some more material, bear?' he asked, lowering his voice and glancing round to make sure no-one else was listening. '*You* could make the model and if it wins we'll share the money.'

Paddington looked at Mr. Curry doubtfully. He didn't remember Valerie saying anything about there being any actual money prizes, but before he had time to explain this small matter the Browns' neighbour took hold of a loose board in the fence and held it up invitingly.

'You can use my guest room if you like, bear,' he said, beckoning Paddington through the hole. 'After all, you must have somewhere proper to work if we're to win a prize.'

Paddington began to look more and more surprised as he squeezed through the gap in the fence and followed Mr. Curry into his house.

He'd never pictured the Browns' neighbour having any guests at all, let alone keeping a special room for them, and he looked around with interest as Mr. Curry pushed open an upstairs door.

'It's only just been decorated,' said Mr. Curry. 'So don't make a mess. And mind the carpet. It's a new one.'

Opening a cupboard he took out the remains of several rolls of wallpaper. 'You can cut as much as you like off these. It's good, thick stuff. Just the thing for models.'

'If you make a good job of it,' he continued, as he made to leave, 'I may even decide not to say any more about that unfortunate business outside earlier on. And no playing around. There's not much time left if you're to get it to the Television Centre by tomorrow.'

Paddington stared mournfully at the door as it closed behind Mr. Curry. The Browns' neighbour had a habit of twisting things round and then disappearing before anyone else had time to change their minds.

Nevertheless he was a hopeful bear at heart and rather than risk displeasing Mr. Curry any further, he got down to the task in hand.

Pushing the bed to one side he unrolled the paper and carefully pinned adjacent sheets of it together, fastening the ends and various other points in between to the carpet with more pins so that it didn't roll up again.

Something Mr. Curry had said just before he left had triggered off an idea in the back of his mind, and for the next few minutes he was kept very busy drawing lines and marking everything out, before he got down to the important matter of cutting out the exact square he was to work from.

This was the moment Paddington had been waiting for, but strangely enough he found it all much harder than he'd expected. Although Mr. Curry had mentioned his wallpaper was good, thick quality, he certainly hadn't expected it to be quite so difficult to cut.

In Mr. Gruber's book Mr. Fold usually held his paper delicately between thumb and forefinger while he snipped at it with a pair of nail scissors, whereas even kneeling down and using both paws, Paddington was hard put to even make a start with Mrs. Bird's scissors, let alone cut out his square.

But at long last he found himself on the homeward stretch and heaving a sigh of relief as he met up with the beginning mark on the paper, he settled himself down in the middle of the floor to enjoy a well-earned rest.

It was while he was mopping his brow with one paw and idly dipping the other into the jar of marmalade which he kept for emergencies that he suddenly caught sight of a small piece of brownish string sticking up through a slit in the paper.

Mindful of Mr. Curry's warning about being tidy, he carefully licked his paw clean and gave the string a tug.

It was quite a long piece of string – much longer that it had appeared at first sight, and in some strange way it seemed to be connected to other pieces, for when he came to the end, a second piece

popped up; only when he pulled this string it ran at right angles to the first, along the adjacent side of the square. And this, in turn, led to yet another piece.

Paddington looked more and more surprised. It was all rather like a conjuring trick; the more pieces of string he pulled the more appeared, and in no time at all he had quite a large pile by his side.

But it was when he lifted up the paper in order to investigate the matter still further that he received his biggest shock of all, and for a moment he stared at the patch of floor as if he could hardly believe his eyes.

When he'd first pinned the paper down, Mr. Curry's room had been fitted with a new brown and green mottled carpet, which ran from wall to wall and left not a square inch of board showing. Now he appeared to be standing on a sort of island of carpet, surrounded on all sides by a small sea of crinkly brown and green waves made up of hundreds of tiny woollen tufts.

Paddington had been in some unfortunate situations before, but it needed only a moment or so trying to fit the tufts of wool back on to the string and then into the gap between the two pieces of carpet to convince him that this was without doubt one of the worst he could remember, for no matter how he arranged the pile, it was obvious Mr. Curry's carpet would never be quite the same again.

The one bright spot on an otherwise cloudy horizon was the fact that the patch in question came where the bed had been, and after picking up the square of carpet and wrapping it in the remains of the paper, Paddington hastily trundled it back into place and pulled the counterpane down as far as it would go.

He was only just in the nick of time, for hardly had he got the room straight than footsteps sounded outside, and a moment later the door opened and Mr. Curry reappeared.

'I've been having second thoughts about this competition, bear,' he announced.

'That's funny, Mr. Curry,' exclaimed Paddington thankfully. 'So have I!'

'Ha!' Mr. Curry waved a piece of paper in the air. 'I had a feeling you might. That's why I brought this.'

Taking an ink pad from an inside pocket he

opened the lid and held it out in front of Paddington. 'I'd like you to put your paw mark on this, bear,' he said sternly. 'Just to show it's genuine. Then there'll be no arguing afterwards.'

* * *

As the familiar strains of the Blue Peter signature tune filled the air Mr. Curry pulled up Mr. Brown's best armchair and settled himself down in front of the television. 'Would someone pass me the sandwiches,' he called. 'I don't want to miss anything.'

The Browns exchanged glances. 'You're sure you wouldn't like one of us to pop down the market and get you a cake?' asked Mr. Brown sarcastically.

'No, that's alright,' said Mr. Curry. 'I'll make do.'

Fortunately Mrs. Bird chose that moment to draw the curtains, otherwise even Mr. Curry's thick skin might have changed colour had it got in the way of some of the looks being cast in his direction.

The exciting news that Paddington's last-minute efforts had been rewarded and he was among the finalists for the top three prizes had spread like wildfire and the Browns' lounge was crowded for the occasion.

Mr. Brown had arrived home early from the office. Mr. Gruber had shut up his shop extra promptly, and quite a few of Paddington's friends from the market had dropped in; but the arrival of Mr. Curry was something no-one had bargained for and as always his presence was tending to cast a gloom over the proceedings. A gloom which wasn't helped by the fact that the most important item in the programme was obviously being kept until the end.

'I do wish they'd get on with it,' grumbled Mr. Curry, reaching out and helping himself to the last remaining sandwich.

'They certainly know how to build up the tension,' agreed Mrs. Brown.

'There he is!' cried Jonathan, as a wider shot showed Paddington sitting on his suitcase in the middle of a small group at the far end of the studio.

Even as he spoke the picture changed to a closer shot and they had a tantalising glimpse of Paddington raising his hat to the viewers as the camera panned along the faces.

'It's a pity you haven't got colour,' said Mr. Curry.

'It's a pity some people haven't got their own television sets,' snorted Mrs. Bird, removing the empty sandwich plate.

It sounded as though she would have liked to say a good deal more but just then Valerie, John and Peter reappeared on the screen and Valerie led the

way across the studio to where a large paper television camera stood at one end of a long table.

'Well, he hasn't won the prize for the best idea,' said Mr. Brown disappointedly, as the first of the winners was ushered up.

'Nor the best but one,' added Mrs. Brown a moment later as the second prizewinner was announced, and the camera showed a beautifully made paper model of a space capsule.

'I can't look,' said Mrs. Bird, as Valerie consulted her list for the third time. 'It's all too exciting for words.'

'And now,' said Valerie, 'the prize for the most original material goes to . . . Paddington Brown of . . . '

The rest of Valerie's announcement was lost as a great cheer rang round number thirty-two Windsor Gardens.

'We've won!' cried Mr. Curry. 'We've won!'

'*We've* won?' Something in the tone of Mr. Curry's voice made Mr. Brown take his eyes from the screen for a moment. 'What do you mean – *we've* won?'

Mr. Curry waved a piece of paper aloft. 'It's all here in black and white,' he said triumphantly. 'I supplied that bear of yours with the material in exchange for a half share in the prize – he's signed it with his own paw.'

'Do you mean to say,' exclaimed Mrs. Bird, her voice trembling with indignation, 'that you persuaded that young bear to sign away half his winnings? Why if I'd known I would have . . . '

'It was *my* wallpaper,' interrupted Mr. Curry. 'If it hadn't been for my wallpaper he wouldn't have won. You heard what they said – it was for the most original material.'

'I hope you like marmalade then,' said Mr. Brown, giving the others a wink. He pointed to the screen which was showing a close-up picture of Paddington's paws clutching an enormous stone jar. 'That's what he's won!'

'Marmalade!' spluttered Mr. Curry. 'Do you mean to say I gave that bear my best wallpaper in exchange for a jar of marmalade?'

'*Half* a jar,' corrected Mrs. Bird. 'That was the agreement.'

Mr. Gruber gave a cough. 'There's another thing,' he said. 'I caught a glimpse of young Mr. Brown's model a moment ago and I must say it didn't look very much like wallpaper to me.'

'What's that?' Mr. Curry turned his attention back to the television just as John took up the story.

'It may not have qualified for the most original idea,' said John.

'And I wouldn't like to say it's the best made,' continued Peter. 'Very good for paws, though,' he added hastily. 'It must have been pretty difficult doing all the folds.'

'But it's certainly the most original material,' said Valerie, as the camera pulled back to reveal Paddington's entry. 'It's the only model of the B.B.C. Television Centre I've ever seen made entirely out of carpet.'

'*Carpet*!' Mr. Curry jumped to his feet, his eyes nearly popping out as he stared at the screen. '*He's made a Television Centre out of my new carpet*!'

Mr. Brown turned to him as a familiar face appeared on the screen. 'Do be quiet,' he said. 'Paddington's trying to say something.'

'Thank you very much, Miss Singleton,' said Paddington. 'It would have been a lot bigger but I'm afraid Mr. Curry's tufts kept falling out.'

'My *tufts* kept falling out!' bellowed Mr. Curry, beside himself with rage. 'I'll give that bear tufts. I'll . . I'll . . . '

'What ever made you choose carpet as a material?' Valerie asked Paddington. 'It's most unusual.'

Paddington thought for a moment. 'Well, I didn't actually *choose* it,' he admitted, glancing anxiously towards the camera. 'It happened. It's really Mr. Curry's.'

'In that case,' said Peter, 'I think he ought to have a prize as well.'

'Hear! Hear!' agreed Valerie.

'We don't usually award Blue Peter badges to grown-ups,' said John, 'but we'll put one in the post for Mr. Curry today.'

'A *badge*!' bellowed Mr. Curry. 'A Blue Peter *badge*. Pah!'

For once the Browns' neighbour seemed at a loss for words. He stood for a moment glaring at the others as they tried hard to keep from laughing and then he turned and strode out from the room.

'Thank goodness for that!' exclaimed Mrs. Brown amid general agreement, as the sound of the front door being slammed echoed round the house. 'Now perhaps we can watch the rest of the programme in peace.'

'Oh, Lord!' Mr. Brown's face suddenly dropped as he took another look at the model on the screen. 'I've just had a thought. I suppose we shall have to buy him a new carpet. Even if it was an accident we can't just leave it.'

'If it's the one in his spare bedroom,' broke in Mr. Gruber, 'I may be able to help. I happen to know he bought it at a sale in the market. I'll get some more tomorrow and I'm sure I can arrange to have it invisibly mended.'

'I must say,' he added, 'whatever it costs it'll be worth every penny just to be reminded of the look on Mr. Curry's face when he saw young Mr. Brown's model on the television.'

'Perhaps it will teach him a lesson,' said Judy.

'I doubt it,' replied Mr. Brown. 'Some people are born that way.' He began to chuckle as a sudden thought struck him. 'I wonder if he would like to borrow my hacksaw?'

The others looked at him in surprise.

'Well,' continued Mr. Brown, as John, Valerie and Peter closed the programme and the camera began tracking in on Paddington's winning entry, 'fair's fair. If Paddington's going to share his jar of marmalade, the least Mr. Curry can do is share his badge. He'll need a hacksaw to cut it in half!'

'No, No, Mr. Noakes!

Dinner is served–not grub's up'

Peter and I were attending a special one day course at a school for butlers and footmen called 'Personal Services' which is run by an imposing ex-butler called Mr. John.

We'd never actually met a real butler face to face – though we'd seen them at the pictures and on television.

A butler's quite a grand person in his own right – the master of all the servants. Beneath him are cooks, housekeepers and *footmen* – who are sort of butlers' labourers.

Although the butler is the boss – he doesn't have nearly so smart a suit as the footman. The butler wears a short black jacket, striped trousers and a black tie, while the footman is dressed in a magnificent livery with a wing collar and a splendid white bow tie.

I quite liked the footman's suit – and Peter said he didn't mind being the boss, so after I'd got dressed and helped Peter on with his coat, we were ready for an interview with Mr. John.

Knapp – the school's butler – told us he'd enquire if Mr. John was available. We waited discreetly in the hall and heard him say:

'Mr. Noakes and Mr. Purves of "Blue Peter", sir.'

We walked in and stood in front of Mr. John's

1 Pete was the butler who is the boss - but I had the smartest suit.

2 Knapp - the School butler - told Peter how the 'grog tray' is prepared-

elegant desk while he gave us a run down on the general behaviour of a footman and a butler.

'You will wear your suit, and *you* your livery – and appear smart and tidy at all times. I personally would never engage anyone with hair as long as yours . . .'

'I only had it cut this morning,' said Peter, touching his hair where it fell over his collar.

'. . . but in your cases I have made an exception,' continued Mr. John.

'You will always be polite to all the guests, calling them Sir or Madam, My Lord or My Lady, or Your Grace – as the case might be.'

'Everything must be handed on a silver tray – letters, cards, notes, glasses – whatever it is.'

There are very strict lines of demarcation in a stately home. A butler *always* serves the drinks. If a guest asks a footman for a drink, he must ask the butler – and the butler will serve it. The footman would never, ever serve a drink to a guest.

Knapp showed Peter how to look after the 'grog tray', which is butler's slang for the drinks tray. The butler is entrusted with the keys to the wine cellar – and it's his duty to see that all the decanters are kept topped up – and any offensive 'used' glass removed immediately.

In the meantime, Mr. John had gone back to bed so that I could practise how to wake a gentleman up.

I knocked at the bedroom door (you never knock on downstairs doors, but you *do* knock on bedroom doors!) and walked in with the tray. After opening the curtains I said in a polite but firm voice:

'Good morning, sir. Tea is served, sir. How am I doing, sir?'

Mr. John opened one eye.

'Not too badly – now you would take away my dinner suit which I had worn the night before and lay out my clothes for the morning. Then you would polish my shoes and run my bath.'

I was relieved to find he didn't want me to scrub his

3 - and how to polish the silver with his thumb!

back, dress him, and carry him downstairs!

Peter in the meantime was learning how to polish the silver – another butler's job. He was welcome to it, too – because everything has to be polished by hand – or rather by thumb.

Silversmith's rouge is rubbed in to every piece, not by a cloth, but by the butler's thumb. It seemed a bit primitive to me, but Knapp insisted that a good butler's thumb took out the scratches better than any cloth.

Answering the telephone is the footman's job – so Mr. John rang me up to see how I would behave. I was sure I knew all the right words because I had seen them do it on the pictures. I picked the phone up and said in my poshest voice:

'You rang, sir?'

'No, no, no. You must give the telephone number – and the name of your master.'

I tried again. 'This is 246-8007 – Mr. John's residence.'

'May I speak to Mr. John?' said Mr. John.

By now I was beginning to get confused.

'It's for you,' I said.

'No, no, no – you must say – "I'll see if Mr. John is *available*." '

I thought as I'd made his tea, woken him up, laid out his clothes, run his bath and polished his shoes, he'd have so much time on his hands he'd be quite glad to have a word on the telephone! But no!

'I'll see if Mr. John is available,' I said to the telephone.

'Sir,' insisted Mr. John.

Peter and I had had some rigorous instruction on how to wait at table. My day as a waiter at the Hilton Hotel was useful here – but there were extra refinements.

'Always place a plate the right way up in front of the guest – particularly if there's a *crest* on it!'

When Mr. John was satisfied, we were sent for a full dress rehearsal at Marble Hill House in Twickenham. Everyone who calls at the house must be treated with proper respect,' warned Mr. John. 'There must be no familiarity – no matter *who* it may be.'

A butler in a well regulated house like Marble Hill would never ever answer the door himself before 12 noon; so when an elegant Rolls Royce purred up the drive, it was footman Noakes who was sent echoing across the marble hall to open the large front door.

A very smart lady in a hat and fur coat stood on the porch – somehow she looked vaguely familiar.

'Good afternoon, Madam.'

'Good afternoon. I've called to see Lord Marble,' she said.

'I'll see if his Lordship is available – if you'd care to come in.' I'd got that bit right, anyway.

4 I was having a quiet rest in the hall . . .

5 . . . when suddenly there was a ring at the door.

6 A very grand lady gave me her card - 'I'd like to see Lord Marble,' she said.

7 I gave the card to Mr. Purves, who said, 'I'll enquire if the master is "at home".'

8 Peter remembered his instructions - 'Always present everything on a salver'.

9 Peter padded softly towards the master's chair . . . .

10 I gave the lady the message-she turned and walked back to the waiting Rolls Royce . . .

The lady gave me her card – and I went off in search of Mr. Purves.
If a footman is not sure of his master's 'availability' to a caller, he must always check with the butler.
Mr. Purves looked quizzically at the card.
'Miss Valerie Singleton of "Blue Peter"?'
He raised his eyebrows, flung the card on a silver salver, and began the long journey up the great oak staircase towards Lord Marble's study. He'd remembered Mr. John's instruction – everything must be presented on a salver!
I waited discreetly behind a pillar in the hall. I peeped out once or twice to see the grand lady waiting by the door. Once I'd swear she saw me looking at her, but she only turned away.
I heard Mr. Purves' creaking boots plodding down the staircase again. He put the card in his breast pocket and whispered an order that sent me across the hall back to the waiting lady.
'I'm afraid Lord Marble is not at home today, Madam.'
She stood motionless for a moment – then I opened the door.
'Good afternoon,' she said.
'Good afternoon, Madam.'
I watched the Rolls glide away past the laurel garden – through the park and towards the distant road.
Mr. John didn't think we'd done too badly – although he did have one or two notes, like 'a good footman does not try to catch the eye of a lady guest waiting in the hall!'
I quite liked the suit – and Peter quite liked bossing me about – but I don't think we were cut out for the job really!
Val said she very much enjoyed being the grand lady arriving in the Rolls Royce.
I think that accounts for everybody—except Lord Marble – and he was not available for comment.

Collectors' Corner

Are You a Collector?

If so, how do you display your collection? It's easy enough to put stamps and postcards into albums, and coins into cases, but what about holiday souvenirs, miniature dolls and animals, shells, fossils, interesting pebbles and bits of rock?

More often than not they end up pushed into the backs of drawers and cupboards and labelled 'junk' – which is a pity when they could be effectively displayed.

We've arranged part of our 'Blue Peter' collection to give you some ideas – so why not have a look at what you've got. You may well find you have the beginnings of an interesting museum.

You don't need a lot of money to make show-cases and stands. The case we use for small treasures is just the bottoms of plastic detergent bottles covered with sticky-backed plastic (or painted, after removing the lettering with wire wool) and stapled together. If you can't borrow a stapling tool, you could stick the containers together – making sure you leave them overnight so that the glue is firmly set.

The good thing about this idea is that you can easily add to the show-case as your collection grows.

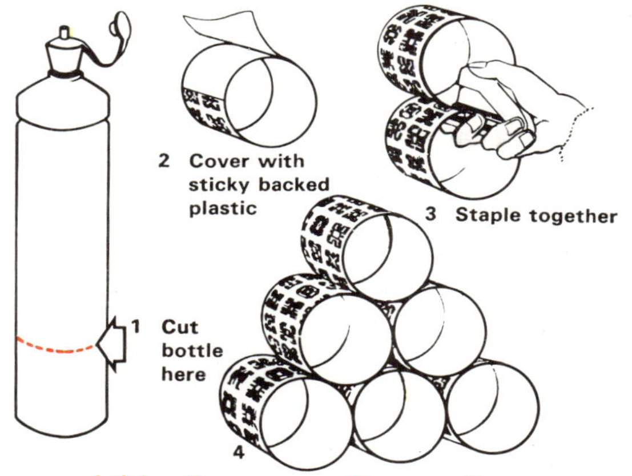

An expandable show-case for small treasures

Shoe boxes and their lids, chocolate boxes, transparent gift boxes, and cardboard egg cartons are all useful containers. The cardboard can be painted or covered with material or sticky-backed plastic – and remember to vary the backgrounds to contrast with the colours of the objects you want to display. Large shells and geological specimens look effective in the hollows of painted egg cartons. Another idea is to group similar things together – like our old watches arranged on a sheet of stiff card. It's also effective to group things on different levels – a flat display tends to look dull.

Cardboard boxes and their lids make useful stands

Try grouping similar things together

Dark objects like these need a light background

An important part of every collection is labelling. Each object should be labelled or catalogued with a brief description, its age, and the date you acquired it. If you have only limited space where labels would take up too much room, why not do what we've done? Stuck underneath each object there's a small piece of paper with a number on it. The numbers correspond to those written in our catalogue book like this:

53 Ammonite BC 180 million years 'Blue Peter' collection 1968

54 Cigar Lights; Original date of manufacture 1871-1916. 'Blue Peter' collection 1968

55 Metal match container. Early 20th Century. 'Blue Peter' collection 1969

Your local museum and library should be able to help identify mystery items, and don't think that some things are too ordinary to keep. As the years go by, what once were everyday objects can become valuable pieces of evidence of Social History. In the museum at Corfe in Dorset, for example, there's an old fashioned chocolate machine that proves you could once buy chocolate in 1d. and 2d. bars – and many other pieces of equipment that show how times have changed.

So keep your eyes open at home and on holiday and see how interesting you can make *your* collection.

Bengo
by Tim
1 Bengo and his friend, Skippy the Scottie, were taken to the seaside one day for a special treat.
BOAT TRIPS
ADULTS 2/-
CHILDREN 1/-
2 When they saw people going on board a boat for a sea trip, they decided to go, too.
3 But the sailor in charge said 'Sorry – no dogs allowed without their owners'.
SEA MIST
4 And a rather snooty dog, sitting in the boat with his owner, laughed at Bengo and Skippy.
5 But further along the beach they saw a boat loaded with crates. 'We can at least take a look on board,' said Bengo.

6 They walked up a little gang plank into the boat. There seemed no harm in what they were doing.
7 Suddenly they heard heavy footsteps behind them - someone was climbing on board! Quickly, Bengo and Skippy hid themselves inside an empty crate, and soon the whole boat was throbbing as the outboard motor started.
8 The next minute they found themselves chugging out to sea. The sailor seemed to be heading for the lighthouse.
9 Bengo and Skippy were swung ashore in a large net – the crates were supplies for the lighthouse keeper!

10 'Come back here!' he called angrily, as the two friends scampered into the lighthouse.
11 But Bengo and Skippy were too scared to stop. They ran up some stone stairs which seemed to go round and round for ever.
12 When they reached a platform with big shining lamps, they found they could go no further. Oh dear, how scared they felt.
13 Just then a friendly face appeared behind them. It was the lighthouse keeper's dog. 'Don't be frightened,' he said.
14 He took Bengo and Skippy to the lighthouse keeper, who turned out to be a really kind man.

15 Picking up a telephone he talked to the coastguard station on the mainland.
16 fifteen minutes later, a bright red helicopter swooped over the sea towards the lighthouse.
17 Bengo and Skippy were winched up in turn into the cabin of the helicopter. They could hardly believe their good luck.
18 Waving goodbye to the lighthouse keeper and his dog, they set off on their flight back to the beach. It was lovely!
19 It was even better when they were landed right by the snooty dog who had laughed at them earlier. Not only had they had a sea trip, but a ride in a helicopter too – quite an adventure for one day.

SWEET OR SAVOURY?

When you invite your friends to tea, what sort of food do they prefer—the sweet things or the savouries? Here are some ideas that should please them all—stuffed dates, savoury eggs and tuna tomatoes. The radish roses and the sausage snacks will help to decorate the table.

Stuffed Dates

You will need: Dates and marzipan; green colouring, nuts; glace cherries and silver balls for decoration. You could also use chocolate chips, angelica or sugar strands. If you hate marzipan, substitute a mixture of equal quantities of butter and sugar creamed together.

Slit along one side of the dates (choosing the least squashy ones) and take out the stones. Divide the marzipan in half – leave half plain and colour the rest with a few drops of green essence or cochineal. Stuff the middles of the dates with marzipan. Decorate.

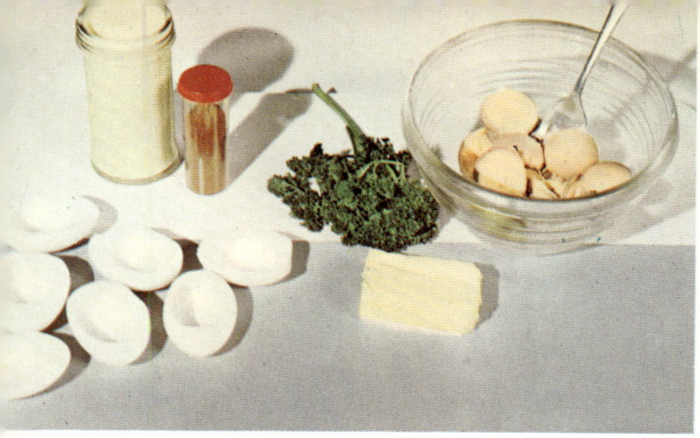 

Savoury Eggs

You will need: Hard boiled eggs; margarine or butter; mayonnaise and seasoning. Parsley and paprika for decoration.

Cut the eggs in half. Mash the yolks with margarine, mayonnaise and seasoning. Fill the eggs with the mixture.

Radish Roses

You will need: A bunch of radishes and a bowl of cold water.
Wash the radishes and trim the stalks. Make 4 or 6 deep crisscross cuts in the top of each one – taking care not to cut right down to the bottom. Put them in a bowl of cold water – after a while they will open like flowers.

Sausage Snacks

You will need: Cold sausages, cheese, capers, cocktail sticks and a grapefruit.
Cut slices of cold sausage and cheese. Spear a slice of cheese, then one of sausage and another piece of cheese onto a cocktail stick. Finish off with a caper. Push the sticks into a grapefruit.

Tuna Tomatoes

You will need: Firm tomatoes (squashy ones are no good); tinned tuna fish (or you can use sardines or pilchards) and seasoning. Water-cress for decoration. A sharp pointed knife.

Mash the tuna with the seasoning. Slice the tops off the tomatoes. Cut a dragon's tooth shape round the edge of each tomato. Scoop out the seeds and fill with tuna.

Biddy Baxter, Edward Barnes and Rosemary Gill would like to acknowledge the help of Gillian Farnsworth and Margaret Parnell.

Designed by Martin Bronkhorst

Answers

Puzzle Pictures

1 American football—John wears the standard outfit for all players.

2 When we had 12-inch high **Sonny Boy** in the studio, he held the record for being the smallest pony in the world.

3 John and Peter dressed up to drive an old **Merryweather** fire engine.

4 This **Hi-lift truck** is a Jumbo Jet loader. The driver can shift $4\frac{1}{2}$ tons of cargo 18 feet in the air without moving from his seat.

5 Unimate, an Industrial Robot, can take a bottle of milk from a refrigerator and pour it into a glass.

6 The 6-foot high head of a giant made especially for Madame Tussaud's Wax Museum. The giant himself was 48 feet tall, and his boots alone reached to the ceiling of the 'Blue Peter' studio.

7 John's unusual mount is **Meppershall Field Marshall**, or Willie for short—a 5 cwt boar.

8 This brass and silver steam locomotive can also be used as a teapot. It was made in Switzerland in 1902.

9 Power Mike, from Biafra, can hold back two minis with the strength of his arms.

10 Piggy, a friendly tapir from Pets Corner at Chessington Zoo.

11 Dum Dum and **Emma**—two baby Indian elephants who came to the studio with their keeper.

12 One of the most valuable chess sets in the world. The figures, made from solid silver and silver gilt, are worth £1,500.

13 Except for its metal framework, this **Cube Car** is made entirely from specially toughened glass. It has a turning circle of only 18 feet.

14 Mr. H. R. Barnard, of Brixton, built this **'Fly Cycle'**. When completed, it will have 49-foot rota blades which he hopes will lift the pilot up into the air.

15 Ted Kelly, joint winner of New Zealand's **'Golden Shears' International Sheep Shearing Championship**.

The Case of the Hi-Jacked Horse

1 The bogus McKinsey said 'back home they'll be celebrating as though it was the 3rd of July'. A real American would know that the Independence Day celebrations take place on the *4th July*.

2 Again, a real American would know that Kennedy Airport is in New York and not in Washington as McKinsey stated.

3 If McKinsey really was a famous horse owner, he would know that the Derby is a flat race, not a steeplechase.

4 Whitby Stevens admitted to meeting Eastower & McKinsey at Badminton the previous week, but McKinsey had said he'd never been in England before and the tannoy announcement stated that Elliot Eastower was appearing for the first time in this country.

5 Had McKinsey been an experienced owner and trainer, he would have known that to give a bucket of cold water to a sweating horse would be disastrous.

Acknowledgements

All photographs in this book were taken by Charles Walls, with the exception of the following:—
No. 7 of the Puzzle Pictures (page 4) by permission of 'The Sun'; Khan (page 8) by Derek Davis; Parachuting (page 9) and film strip (page 11) by Captain G. C. P. Shea-Simonds; Seals (page 12 & 13) from *A Guide to Seals in the Public Record Office* (HMSO). (Wykeham's Seal for New College reproduced by courtesy of the Warden and Fellows of the College); FA Cup Photographs (page 18) by the Football Association; Daniel (page 21) by Joan Williams; Pavlova as '*The Swan*' (page 51) from Radio Times Hulton Picture Library; other photographs (page 51 & 52) from *Pavlova* by A. H. Franks, pub. Burke. Her shoes were loaned by the London Museum.

'A Star Danced' was written by Dorothy Smith. Inside the Fowler BB1 by Geoffrey Wheeler.

The Little Musician was illustrated by Robert Broomfield; Bengo, Bleep & Booster and the Mystery Picture by 'Tim'. The Case of the Hi-jacked Horse was illustrated by Bernard Blatch. The FA Cup illustrations by Michael Whittlesea.

Blue Peter Competition

Would you like to meet Valerie, John, Peter and the rest of the 'Blue Peter' team? Would you like to see all the animals? Would you like to come to London and have tea with them all?

This is your chance!

How long have you been a 'Blue Peter' viewer? If you've seen each programme since we very first started, by now you could be grown up! Using this as a clue – we want you to answer the questions on the entry form.

The First Prizes will be an invitation to an exciting

Blue Peter Party

and there will be lots of competition badges for all the runners up, too.

First Prize winners and runners-up will be notified by letter. The closing date for entries is 12th January, 1970.

Send your entry form to : Blue Peter (Competition), BBC Television Centre, London W.12

Entry Form

If I'd watched every single 'Blue Peter' up to Christmas 1969

1 Altogether I'd have seen__________________programmes

2 Approximately__________________words would have been spoken

3 All the programmes put together would last for__________________hours

Signed __________________ Age ________

Address ____________________________________

____

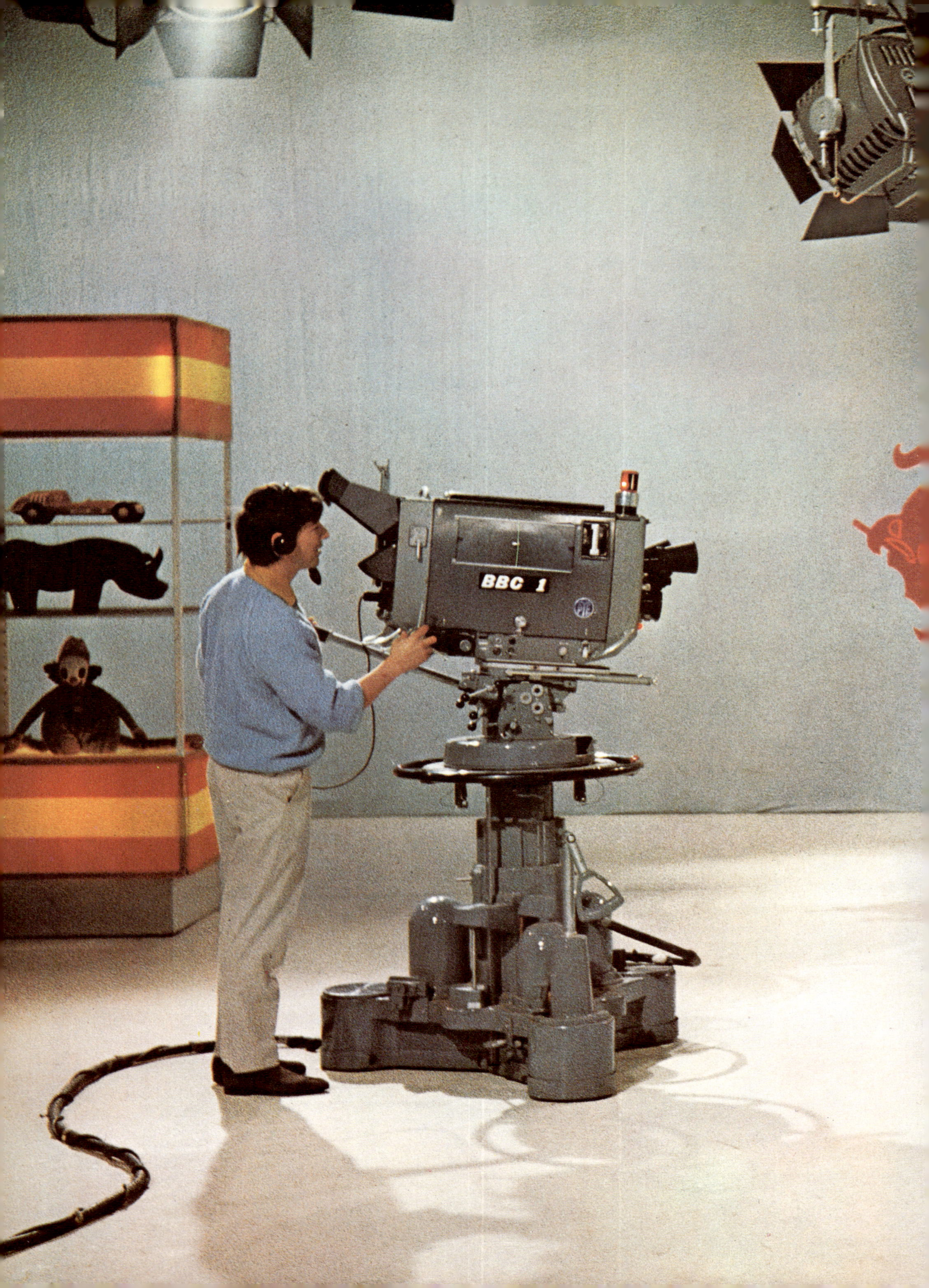
BBC 1